WOMAN
IN ANCIENT AFRICA

by Heinrich Loth

Translated from the German by Sheila Marnie

Lawrence Hill & Company
Westport, Connecticut

© 1987 Edition Leipzig
Published in the English language
for exclusive distribution
in the United States and Canada
by Lawrence Hill and Company
Westport, Connecticut 06880 – 1987
ISBN 0-88208-218-3
Drawings and design: Sonja Wunderlich
Produced by Druckerei Volksstimme Magdeburg
Printed in the German Democratic Republic

Contents

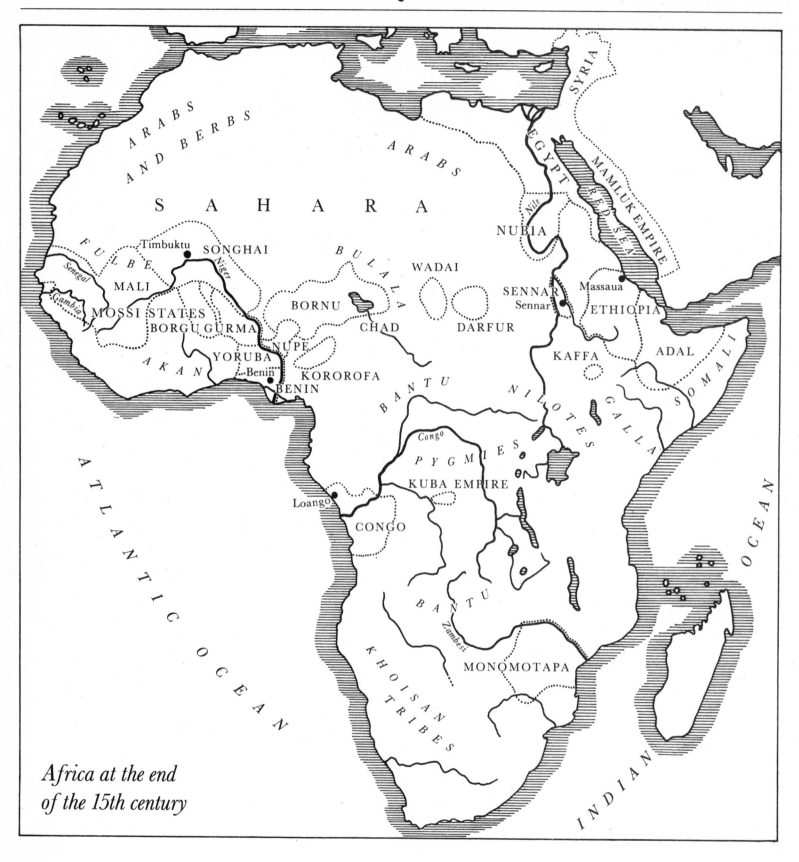

*Africa at the end
of the 15th century*

Foreword

In old reports travellers give enthusiastic accounts of, among other things, the external appearance of the African women. There was no lack of "classical forms"—whereby, in a eurocentric way, the ancient Hellenist ideal of beauty was used as the point of comparison: the graceful movement of their bodies was praised, the peculiar charm of their facial expressions, in short, their entire appearance. Often an imaginative picture of their lack of morals and shamelessness was presented at the same time, a penomenon which made the miscomprehension of African customs evident.

In more recent times, the African woman has less frequently been the subject of historians and cultural historians, but, with the exception of serious ethnographic publications, has tended to figure in works of so-called sexual research, the results of which are published in books full of lavish illustrations.

In this book, a predominantly cultural-historical picture will be presented of the former kingdoms in Africa to the south of the Sahara, in which the role of certain outstanding individual female figures will be examined, as well as everyday life in the country and the towns. An attempt will be made to pay tribute to the untiring and creative activity of the African woman as wife, mother, child-rearer, in her daily work or in a specialized trade.

The old sources will often be allowed to speak for themselves; the numerous travellers' reports which have hitherto not been evaluated from the point of view of the position of women. Even the illustrations to these tales are a rich source of information. Cave drawings and archaeological finds provide further authentic evidence, in this way helping us towards a better understanding of African conditions.

The choice and interpretation of quotations have been based on their historical, regional and social representativeness. Anything of a chance character has been ignored, in order to avoid unwarranted generalizations. This was particularly important, because Africa to the south of the Sahara experienced a strong process of diversification in the centuries described.

Gentile social relations coexisted with socially and economically advanced early feudal class societies within organized states. Gatherers, hunters and farmers lived next to nomadic shepherds. Early black African kingdoms existed next to Islamic systems of government, and often all these elements coexisted in a kind of interwoven pattern. This multi-layeredness and cultural diversity have to be taken into account when considering the social and legal position of women.

The colonial period was a difficult one for the peoples of Africa, and particularly for women. The emergence of the Dark Continent as a supplier of goods and raw materials, the phenomenon of migrant labour, and the spread of export-oriented economies, all served to undermine the traditional systems of work-relations and family life. The subordination of women to men was gradually consolidated, even if some of their special rights were retained in some areas right down to the 19th and 20th centuries. At present the question of women is closely linked with the development situation in general, and an understanding of present-day problems requires an investigation of the history of African women.

I was given much valuable support in preparing this book. My thanks go to numerous museums and libraries, but especially to the Forschungsbibliothek in Gotha. I would also like to thank Dr. Suckow and Professor Dr. Woelffing for their advice.

Heinrich Loth

Introduction

"It is certainly true that the African woman was, among other things, a worker and a source of additional manpower in the fields of a polygamist. She was used now and then as an exchange good or a dowry gift, as a way of strengthening social ties.

But despite the physical mutilations sometimes imposed on her, the African woman also enjoyed certain privileges. These were in contradiction to her oppression, and gave her an enviable position in comparison to women in other countries during the same period.

Quite honestly the African woman was ... a lively, irrepressible source of optimism. There was nothing happier than a group of women who had gathered to collect wood, bring in the harvest, or grind, sort and prepare millet. As producers of goods and of children, as priestesses and as lovers, African women always sang the lullaby of the peoples as they went about their daily chores, experienced their misfortunes, hopes and fears, joys and pleasures."

Joseph Ki-Zerbo

Ancient empires, iron-age civilizations, and a flourishing artistic life had all existed in the part of Africa to the south of the Sahara long before its first contact with Europeans. Anyone looking at the history of this part of the world stumbles across reports of large and powerful African states and finds that the sources for the history of this area always come up with new puzzles but also with amazing new information. Africa to the south of the Sahara experienced a simultaneous upswing in the economic, political and cultural life of most of its territories from the end of the 12th to the end of the 16th century. Joseph Ki-Zerbo was the first African to give a complete historical presentation in his book *The History of Black Africa*. In it he writes: "These four centuries really deserve to be called the great epoch of Black Africa ... This manifested it-

self in the high-ranking social organizations which brought these countries nearer to the rest of the world." (96) This development did not, however, begin out of the blue; great kingdoms had existed in this area before the 12th century.

The civilizations throughout Africa grew out of these roots, and this common cultural heritage lasted for centuries. It provided a common historical experience and remained the basis for an African cultural unity which was retained despite the undoubted differences within it. If, in what follows, North Africa and Egypt appear to be neglected, this is due to the sources and literature available: these differ considerably between the north and south of the continent. It is also because the role of women in the area to the south of the Sahara was very different to that of women in the North African areas, which were strongly influenced by Islamic culture.

Just as the numerous African peoples and tribes went through different stages of socio-economic development and present a confusing picture of ethnic and cultural variety, so, too, did the way of life of the two sexes, and their relationship with each other vary enormously from region to region. Within the variety of social relations, even between neighbouring peoples, the position of women displayed its own particular characteristics. Whereas in one part of the continent the social oppression and exploitation increased, in another part the remnants of matrilinear rights persisted stubbornly. Moreover, some peoples clung on to a tradition in their social life whereby the men had a slightly lower status and women dominated. This was a source of great surprise to the first European travellers to Africa.

Of course, one can only ever speak of the main strands in historical development, or of basic features. In many cases, only typical examples can be given, often extrapolated from different territorial conditions, from contradictory and complex socio-economic processes and historical developments. The matrilinear gentile legal system existed alongside the patrilinear

1

Bowl with kneeling
woman for the Ifa Ora-
cle. Wood. Height
23 cm. Yoruba, Nigeria.
Rietbergmuseum, Zurich.

2

This depiction of a mother and child testifies to the high degree of sophistication of African art. There are quite clearly demarcated stylistic traditions according to region. Mother with child. Height 56 cm. Northwest Baluba, eastern Congo area. Rietbergmuseum, Zurich.

3

The human body is usually depicted in a standing position; seated, squatting or kneeling figures are rarer. This seated woman displays, in addition to abstract features, disproportionate dimensions and a certain rigidity of expression which has a powerful effect on the observer. Seated woman. Height 39 cm. Malinke, Guinea. National Museum of Denmark, Copenhagen.

4

Most figures appear on their own, groups are exceptional. Where the latter do occur, the mother and child motif is commonest. Statuette of a woman carrying a child on her back. Dan, West Africa. Musée national, Paris.

5

Masks in various forms served, among other purposes, that of handing down rituals and customs. One can differentiate between face-masks, hand-held masks, and ones fitted over the head. Every real mask should also have a clothing to go with it. Female mask. Museum für Völkerkunde, Vienna.

6

Traditional works of art usually have a blackish surface. A variety of features serve both to differentiate the historical-cultural regions from each other as far as masks are concerned and also to allow comparisons to be made. Female figure. Wood, shiny, relatively light brown patina. Height 32 cm. Ngbaka. Staatliches Museum für Völkerkunde, Linden-Museum, Stuttgart.

7

Vessels in the form of a human head or a female figure were regarded as particularly prestigious. Depictions of women in connection with everyday artefacts were probably the result of a need to gain such prestige. Calabash. Clay. Mangbetu, Zaïre. Tropical Museum, Amsterdam.

8

Art served not only religious cults but also the need to achieve prestige. For the African tradition it is not possible to make the differentiation between craft-objects and works of art that is common in Europe. Chief's stool, supported by kneeling woman. Wood. Height 58 cm. Luba, Zaïre. Staatliches Museum für Völkerkunde, Linden-Museum, Stuttgart.

9

Masks such as this one
from the grasslands of
Cameroon were worn
during dances at funer-
als. Length 71.5 cm,
width 63 cm. Museum für
Völkerkunde, Leipzig.

10

According to the function
which they had, masks
could depict mythical
characters, spirits or demons, but also ancestors.
They were used by the
secret societies. Sowei
mask from the female
secret society Sande.
Dark, stained wood.
Height 40 cm. Mende,
Sierra Leone. Histo-
risches Museum, Bern.

The ruined palace of "Ta'akha Mariam" in Ethiopia from the 3rd to 5th centuries demonstrates the sheer size of such buildings. After the collapse of the Aksum Empire in the 10th century, elements of the architecture of these earlier buildings were taken over in the style of Christian churches in Ethiopia. Institut für Denkmalpflege, Berlin (Frobenius Collection).

14

Towns differed from villages in appearance usually only in their size and importance as craft, trading and cultural centres. This remained the case right into the 19th century. View of the town of Aksum. Institut für Denkmalpflege, Berlin (Frobenius Collection).

one; the decline of gentile social systems took place at the same time as early feudal systems were taking shape. However, the advantage of presenting an over-all picture is that it conveys a living image of the role of women in the history of old Africa, and of the changes which took place over the centuries. It gives one the opportunity to break with the preconceptions about the African woman in the pre-colonial era, according to which, in general, she had a completely subserviant role.

In the period between the 12th and 16th centuries, which is the period to which we will devote most attention, there existed large and powerful African empires, the history of which is documented in archaeological finds, myths, and chronicles, and also in the extremely interesting work of Arabian and European writers. After a period of rapid cultural development, powerful kingdoms were founded by the peoples of the western Sudan, Senegal and the Niger basin, the Guinea coast and the Congo basin. This was a period of state-creation which lasted from the 8th century and reached a temporary peak in the 13th century. It was the forerunner of·a great epoch which lasted from the 12th to the end of the 16th century; a period in which "the black African countries achieved a certain degree of equilibrium after a phase of migrations, of contact and exchange with the outside world mediated by the Arabs, some of which was beneficial, and after a demographic upswing". (96)

The social development of the African peoples reached a higher or lower level depending on concrete historical conditions: sooner or later they changed from the norms of matrilinearity to those of patrilinearity. This was a long drawn out process, which is documented not only by the history of the old kingdoms but also by the lives of many peoples and tribes where the remnants of a matrilinear society could be observed until very recently. With the growth in power of the elders and heads of the big families and of the chiefs and kings over the ordinary tribe members, and more particularly with the development of

early feudal relations, conditions were created which did not have a favourable effect on the position of women. The situation became worse with the development of towns. Women, particularly those from socially privileged strata, were more or less cut off from the rest of society.

The reason that remnants of the matrilinear societies could be observed until the 16th century, and even in the very recent past, is that there was such a variety of socio-economic conditions. Within the context of the ancient kingdoms, groups of tribes went through the most diverse stages of development. In every new socio-economic formation, even in the feudal one, the ethnic characteristics of the previous epoch continued to exist alongside those inherent in the new one. Analogous processes whereby groups, which had retained many features of primitive society and of the original matrilinear relations, were incorporated into larger units can be followed in other parts of the world. A considerable proportion of the people living south of the Sahara did not yet know the class society. Many peoples and tribes still lived in gentile relations. Some were just developing into states, and others were developing within the framework of slave or feudal states. The following centres can be clearly identified within the processes of state-formation:

1. The area which today constitutes Ethiopia, the oldest state, the core area of which dates back to the 1st century B.C. Even in the time of Antiquity there was an empire here. This was the Aksum Empire at the beginning of the 4th century A.D. where Orthodox Christianity was introduced spreading all over the country until c. 1500.

The Christian religion began to develop in Africa quite early on. From the middle of the 2nd century onwards, Judean-Christian communities began to emerge in Alexandria and other cities in North Africa. Their influence spread as far as Carthage. It is worth remembering that the story of Joseph and Moses took place partly in Africa, that the Septuagint, the Greek translation of the Old Testament, was completed on

African soil, and that Africa (in particular Ethiopia) became the refugee camp for exiled Christians.

Some of the most famous names from ancient Christianity were to be found in Africa: Origines, Cyprian, Tertullian, Augustine. Many other outstanding theologians were active here. Whereas the Christian church in Egypt and in the rest of North Africa was almost eliminated through the wave of Arabian conquests which began in 640 A.D., in Ethiopia and the Sudan it survived the Islamic onslaught and remained a leading religious force over the centuries.

2. West Africa. The Nok culture is a puzzling one. It is named after the site where life-size figures and fragments of figures were found. It developed from about 500 B.C. until 200 A.D. in what is now the territory of Nigeria. It has become increasingly clear that it had a great influence on the ancient peoples of Africa. The terracotta sculptures of this culture are the oldest of all known sculptures in West Africa. A number of peoples, including the Yoruba, are the descendants of this civilization. Most of the ethnic groups in the territory which was once under the influence of the Nok have retained a great similarity in culture and religion over the centuries and even until the present.

In West Africa the early states are said to have been formed in the period from the 3rd century A.D. (old Ghana) until the 13th century (rise of the Hausa states). Their formation may, however, have begun earlier.

Long before Islam began to take root in the 7th century, the characteristic and peculiarly African brand of Christianity had been firmly established in the apostolic era in the whole of North Africa, in Egypt, Ethiopia, and parts of the Sudan. It is highly probable that it even spread to West Africa in these bygone times.

The Ghanaian Empire, which lasted until the mid-13th century, played a role as a transit route and exchange market for Mediterranean trade. There were direct caravan routes from Ghana to Ethiopia, Egypt, and Nubia. The old Empire of Kanem (8th to 12th century) stretched at its peak from the Niger to the Nile, and it even influenced Egypt. Other states succeeded the Kanem Empire after its demise in 1200. Apart from these, the states of Mali, Songhai, and Bornu were formed in the 1st millennium.

The Mandingo tribes were responsible for the foundation of several states. The most important ruler was Mandi Mansa (1308–1332). He held court in Timbuktu. The famous traveller Ibn Battuta, who visited Timbuktu in 1352, expressed wonder at the ruler's palace. Mandi Mansa began a pilgrimage to Mecca in 1326, and this was the most resplendent pilgrimage ever made by an African king. Numerous other states were founded at the estuary of the Senegal, on the upper reaches of the Niger and in other regions. The Hausa states are worth mentioning: their history began more than 1,000 years ago. Kano, the most important Hausa Empire, had active trade connections with places as far away as Tunis.

In 1446 the powerful empire of the Wolof was established. By 1600 it had, however, already disintegrated into small successor states. The state of Ashanti also had an ancient tradition. The empire was ruled by a king, who resided in Kumasi. Apart from him there was a Council, composed of head-priests, provincial governors, army leaders, court officials and some of the king's relatives. The ruler was bound by the approval of the Council in all important matters. The most important symbol of state was a golden throne, which was always protected by a royal guard. In West Africa, the states in Dahomey (founded by the Ewe), some states in the land stretching from Togo to Lake Chad, and the Benin Empire (with a civilization which dates back to Antiquity), deserve to be mentioned.

In West Africa, craftwork was already separated from agriculture and reached a very high standard. The production of textiles and metal processing developed into independent spheres of activity. In some places, the beginnings of a credit and money system could even be detected.

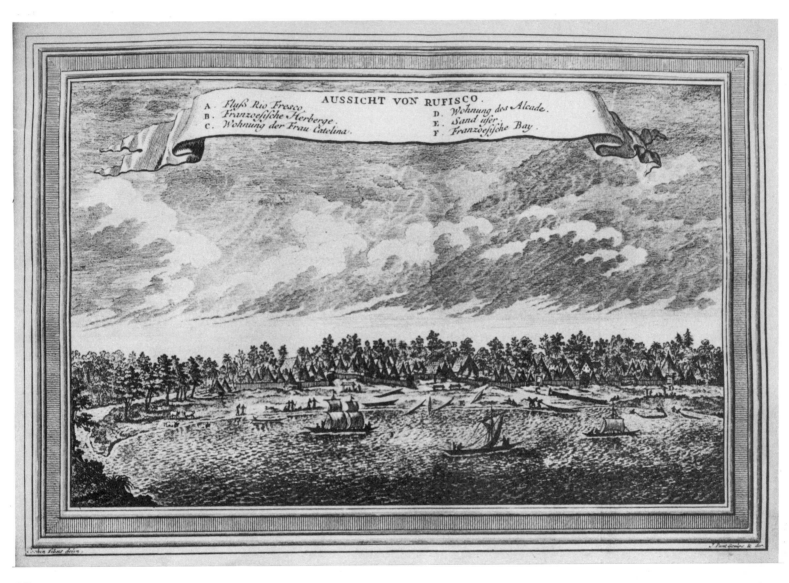

17

This view of Rufisco shows typical architectural features. From:
General History of Voyages by Land and Sea ..., Leipzig 1747.
Forschungsbibliothek Gotha.

3. The Congo Empire, which attracted the attention of the European courts from the end of the 15th century onwards. In 1491 the king had already let himself be baptized, and had renamed the capital, Ambassi, as San Salvador. From the 15th century, there existed in the Congo region the Lunda Empire, which was ruled by a king, Mwata Yamvo, and his wife, Lukokesha, his co-regent. Without any outside influences, a small goods economy flourished in this state and a common currency was introduced.

4. East Africa. The foundation of the Niamwesi state was of prime importance here. However, other tribes also deserve a mention, in particular the Masai and the Kikuyu. There was an empire in Uganda which can be traced back into Antiquity. The king was surrounded by a court state and many officials. There was a throne in the regal hall on which the emperor granted audiences. The hall was lined by the priestesses who accompanied the king. The military was impressive. Every man was a warrior. Every troop had its own battle march and its own priestesses, who performed religious ceremonies before battle.

5. South Africa. There were ancient empires in this area as well, although much less is known about them. When the Portuguese reached the Zambesi in the 16th century they heard tales of a great African empire, Monomotapa, which was supposed to be half way up the Zambesi. This empire was surrounded by legend, and it left a unique memento of itself in the famous ruined town of Zimbabwe, where the remains of many grandiose, old-fashioned stone constructions, old mines, furnaces for melting metal, hand-crafted tools made of iron, copper, bronze, zinc, and gold, clay moulds for copper coins, wells, canals, and walled terraces were discovered, as well as thousands of old gold, copper, iron, and zinc finds. The empire reached the peak of its power from the 12th to the 16th century. More was known about the formation of the Zulu state in South Africa; also about that of the Ndebele and the Shona. A common currency was likewise introduced early on in South Africa.

The process of early state formation was accompanied by socio-economic changes, and changes in the role of women in social life and the family economic unit. There is no doubt that many of the old habits, customs and traditions disappeared with time. Overall, an order based on a shared economy, proved to be increasingly incompatible with the concern of the heads of the individual families to have personal control over property and the right to pass this on to their children. In a number of areas which today belong to Nigeria, Kenya, Uganda and other countries this disintegration of gentile society was far advanced. In East and West Africa there were early feudal conditions under which women, together with other classes in society, had to suffer. "The state was divided into unequal social classes ... around Gao, Timbuktu and Djenne groups of serfs of the Asikia or prisoners of big traders worked the land for their owners. Women formed a particularly oppressed class." (96) In northern Sudan Islam had established itself, in Ethiopia there was an ancient African line of Christianity.

In addition to the variety of socio-economic conditions, there was a further reason why matrilinearity persisted well beyond the 16th century. This was the character of the division of labour between the sexes whereby the woman played an important role in the running of the household and in other spheres. This reason, in addition to the strength of old traditions and customs, should be stressed, because it determined the rights of women through the ages and gave them certain privileges which they were able, despite all odds, to maintain right down to the present day in a number of areas of Africa. Our sources are provided, above all, by reports of travellers who, since Ibn Battuta, the famous Islamic traveller (1304–1377), have given us large numbers of accounts in Arabic, and, since the 15th century, by Italian, Portuguese, Dutch, French and British authors. All of them confirm the impressions of Ki-Zerbo. In evaluating these travellers' reports it becomes clear that many cultural-historical aspects—not least those concerning the life of women—were still discernible in later centuries and are described excellently by some travellers. Some of them even point to their ancient origins. Ki-Zerbo wrote about the privileges of the African women as follows: "Such special rights included great sexual freedom, in some animistic countries even pre-marital freedom; the freedom to go their own way with regard to maternity and family visits; a particularly strong link with their children, since they had to devote themselves entirely to the children during their first years; matrilinearity giving their brother authority over their children; economic freedom through the profits of their various agricultural and trading activities, especially in the coastal regions, but also in Hausa territory; political and intellectual rights, which could even open up the path to a throne or regency, or could mean that they became respected priestesses, especially for fertility rites." (96)

In evaluating the European travel reports it should not be forgotten that the authors of the 16th and 17th centuries were witnessing the fall of the great African empires. The main factor contributing to this was the growing slave trade and the break or fall in trade with Egypt and the Orient, as well as the beginnings of colonial policies. The great empires such as, for example, ancient Ghana, Mali, Songhai, and the Hausa states were replaced by new states the ruling stratum of which often joined forces with the slave traders.

Only when the early political, socio-economic, cultural and other achievements of the African peoples have been given due recognition can the role of the woman in ancient Africa be appreciated today. Only then does it become clear that her position compared favourably in many respects to that of the woman in medieval Europe.

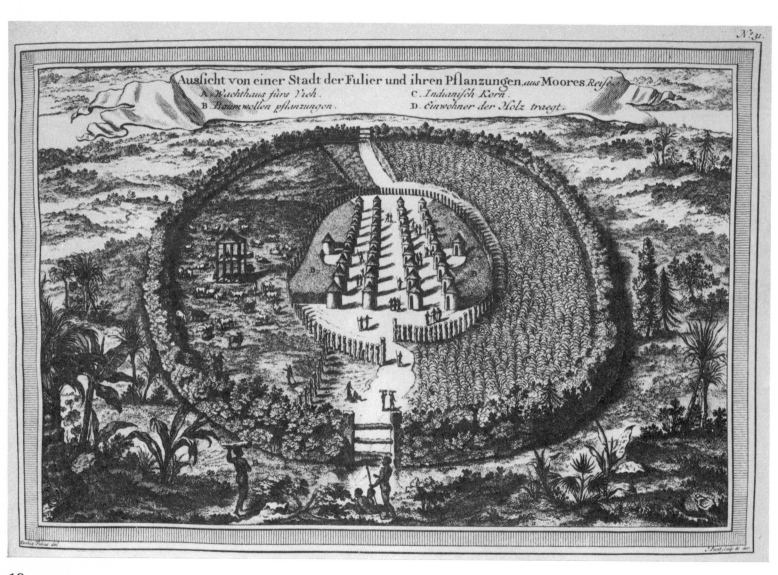

Ausficht von einer Stadt der Fulier und ihren Pflanzungen, *aus* Moores *Reyse*
A. *Wachthaus fürs Vieh.*   C. *Indianisch Korn.*
B. *Baumwollen pflanzungen.*   D. *Einwohner der Holz traegt.*

18

This West African town displays an ordered layout of the houses and
the fields surrounding them. From: *General History of Voyages by Land
and Sea ...*, Leipzig 1747. Forschungsbibliothek Gotha.

THE LEGAL SITUATION

Matrilinearity — patrilinearity

The living arrangements of the extended family in peasant cultures often took the form of a complex of individual huts, many of these consisting only of one room: one for the head of the family, others for the wives and children, cooking, animals etc. Even in towns most of the buildings were of this nature.

The women built the huts, worked in the fields, pounded the rice and corn and did the cooking; the men attended council meetings, sat and drank beer together, waged wars, went hunting and fishing and otherwise lazed around, allowing their "female staff" to serve them. This is the sort of description commonly given of the division of labour which existed in pre-colonial Africa. This sort of exaggerated generalization is not, however, upheld by the facts, and old travel accounts contain many reports which lead to quite different conclusions. In many tribes the men also helped to cultivate the fields and look after the animals, indeed, the raising of animals was, in the case of the shepherd-nomads regarded as the exclusive prerogative of the men. The Islamic scholar Ibn Battuta has given a very typical description of the roles taken by the two sexes—a description which has the additional merit of dating from very early times (1352/1353). In Timbuktu, at the time an important centre in Mali, he observed, with some surprise, that women "were treated with more respect than men". Relations between men and women struck the scholar/traveller as being "unusual".

With the development of the old kingdoms, matrilinearity or at least important aspects of it, were preserved. Matrilinearity and patrilinearity are taken, in their widest sense, to be equatable with matriarchy and patriarchy. In a matrilinear system, descent and inheritance follow the female line, in a patrilinear system the male line. In communities organized according to matrilinearity, the children belonged to the relatives of the mother and inherited material goods as well as economic, social and religious duties from their relatives on their mother's side; males inherited mainly from the mother's brother. This was the case in the kingdom of Mali in the 14th century, where the female line predominated, as can be seen from Ibn Battuta's report about Timbuktu. The men "show no signs whatsoever of jealousy; none of them calculate their descent from their father, but rather from their mother's brother. The heirs of a man are the sons of his sister and not his own sons. I have never witnessed anything similar anywhere in the world except among the Indians of Malabar. The latter are heathens, but the former are Moslems, who adhere assiduously to their set hours for prayer, study the Law and learn the Koran by heart." (1)

Matrilinearity, which is not necessarily the same thing as female dominance, but was often linked with this, had a determining influence on the development of society in the prehistorical period. This was a period during which both sexes had to contribute equally to the task of survival. The male was the hunter, the female the gatherer; the female also looked after the household and the family and saw to it that food was distributed fairly. A matrilinear system was not based on subordination but rather on cooperation and harmonious development. This basis was also determined by the primitive state of development of the factors of production, the weakness of the material basis for production and the constant need for them to deploy all their forces simultaneously. From generation to generation, faced with only a very slight division of labour between man and woman based merely on natural factors, both sexes had to fight hard for their bare survival.

Matrilinearity thus was typical of an economic and cultural stage of development which was largely characterized by an economy based on gathering, hunting and fishing. The females, by gathering wild fruits, herbs and grasses made an important contribution. They thus became the "inventors" of agriculture, which brought with it further innovations, such as the first major example of a social division of labour—the division into tribes which were non-nomadic cultivators and those which were pastoral nomads. According to the degree to which there was a greater tendency towards nomadism or towards cultivating and the degree to which wealth was accumulated and property differentials grew, matrilinearity was now replaced by patrilinearity. The British ethnographer P. Rattray, who made a detailed study of the customs and lifestyle of the Ashanti of West Africa, traced the way in which the power and authority of the oldest male (usually the oldest brother) grew over all other relatives, including unmarried females. (124) This increased authority, accompanied by a widening wealth differential must have led to a clash with the interests of the family of the male. In contrast to a matrilinear system, a patrilinear one, with its allocation of a preeminent position to a male as absolute head of a family group, such as occurred, in particular, in the case of the patriarchal extended family, aimed at putting women in a subordinate position.

Since the beginning of the 1st century A.D., agriculture had been coming to the forest areas of West Africa. A production surplus became commonplace and this formed the basis for property rights and various forms of exploitation. The development of agriculture and animal husbandry made the emergence of an early form of class structure possible. By the 15th century it was the peoples of the western Sudan, Senegal and the Niger Basin and the Guinea Coast who had developed this furthest—even if this region was not the only one to produce important African kingdoms.

In the central part of Ethiopia, northern Sudan, Nigeria, Kenya or Uganda, where early feudal conditions developed, the position of women worsened considerably over the years. Thus in parts of Cameroon the fields belonging to rich peasants and village elders were tilled in most cases by women. In addition, every peasant woman had to give the village chief one basket of the grain which she had harvested from her field. Among other peoples there was a custom whereby each year women had to spend the first day in the fields working for the village chief. Reports from travellers and missionaries in southern Africa mention services rendered by poor women tilling the fields for richer peasants, in particular for the chiefs of tribal units; further the handing over of agricultural produce to these is mentioned, and the hiring of women from the "poorer classes" by "rich persons" for work on the land. (130)

The settling of questions of descent and the change of inheritance from the maternal to the paternal line did not occur precisely at the same time as this progress in production. In the more progressive socio-economic circles there was a special development of the matrilinear structures in families and ethnic-social units. Here women took over the role of head of the family or even queen. This position as queen was a common exception to the rule, an example of matriarchy meaning not only matrilinearity but also female dominance. Earlier or existing family structures based on matrilinearity determined the line of succession. Thus, in the kingdom of Congo and in other African states, the tradition persisted of determining the line of succession according to the female side, even when the candidate was male. For example, H. C. Monrad, reporting on his visit to West Africa in 1805–9, wrote: "One of the strange customs in Ashanti and in the kingdom of Augna is that of the son of the king's sister, not the son of the king himself, being first in line of succession. The blacks believe that this is more likely to ensure that the succession remains in the family than if the more usual method is used." (36)

It should be remembered that in such early feudal conditions the ethnic communities which emerged co-existed with older groupings which still survived. This fact has to be given due consideration in connection with the topic we are concerned with here. In the final phase of the unified formation of primitive society with a pre-gentile and a gentile era, and also in the phase of early feudalism, there existed communities with differing structures, "which led to a multi-layered ethnic consciousness". Different groups of tribes could be absorbed into the old kingdoms, including both those in which the transition to a state had already occurred and those whose social structure was of a much more primitive nature. An exact differentiation between late primitive societies and the formation of early class systems, between gentile elements and the early feudal state, and not least between stagnation and a retrograde development under outside influences—all these factors are of vital importance for the interpretation of the life of women.

Every village community, depending on the natural economy, the degree of economic autonomy, had a specific tribal consciousness. "With many peoples, particularly the nomads, such a local sense of identity included remnants of a tribal or even a gentile consciousness. In addition, however, they possessed a clear consciousness of belonging to larger territorial groupings, of being part of the population of a specific country which—if in form alone—possessed an ultimate ruler, a prince, king or emperor." (134) Under the influence of external factors—particularly when

these coincided with periods of feudal fragmentation—once powerful kingdoms disintegrated and a period of stagnation and retrograde development set in, as occurred after the 16th century with the onset of colonial-feudal and colonial-capitalistic influence, when continuity of development in Africa was suddenly interrupted.

It is undoubtedly true to say that changes in the social position of women had more specific social causes than merely the ever-increasing division of labour, social differentiation and the rise of male property rights: the increasing physical demands made on those involved in working on the land or, later on, the necessity of specific training qualifications for those taking up urban professions also played an important role in this process.

What role was played by religion in the relationship of matrilinearity to patrilinearity? The central question which arose at an early stage in the history of human civilization and religion also arose in African religions: How was the world created? How was Man created? What happens to him after death? Africa was rich in myths which explained the Creation, the division of heaven and earth, the creation of Man, the origins of each tribe and its first appearance in a particular geographical area. Many African tribes could trace their origins back to a famous female ancestor. Even those which had long since changed to a patrilinear system had a lineage going back to the tribal mother. The important role played by women is clearly illustrated by this.

Originally the fertile earth, the moon, which according to old beliefs influenced the earth, and the element water were female, whereas fire and the sun were male. In the tribal myths the easily comprehensible symbolism of gender associated with the elements and heaven, earth, moon and sun were subject to change, but matrilinearity in its many remnants survived and was preserved in mythology—often a highly concise oral tradition—and in various ancient religious forms.

The qualitative change in economic and cultural conditions marked by the development from a gathering, hunting and fishing culture to one using digging-stick and hoe to cultivate the land and involving animal husbandry received expression, amongst other places, in religion. The primitive religions characteristic for African peoples just after or during the first stage of development became polytheistic beliefs in which ancestor-worship and fetishism were preserved. Animism, the belief in the spiritual life of animate and inanimate objects, together with the belief in magic forces, both survived. The supernatural world of African tribes, which hitherto had consisted of a fairly undifferentiated mass of formless gods now became much more clearly defined and a belief emerged in a supreme divinity, several gods and goddesses with various specific functions and spheres of influence. Just like in the "major" religions, so now mythological beliefs traced the creation of the world back to a highest Being, a supreme divinity, a Spirit or a Great Mother.

H. Baumann wrote of a dualism of "female earth-goddess" and "male heavenly god", a pair of "world parents" which, between them—this is either made explicit or remains implicit—created the "world". (53) It is interesting to note the characteristics of the two divinities which J. Zwernemann wrote about: "The major characteristic of the earth goddess is that she is a goddess of fertility ... the earth is closely associated with this group and its moral and ethical tenets ... the worship of the earth usually takes place in sacred groves." (141) The heavenly god was an appendage of the earth goddess. He was a creator, a ruler of the universe, standing in judgement over souls. "He is frequently benign, but in some myths he turns out to be a despot." (140) In addition to these two, there are "special" gods and inferior gods, such as the Ewe, Dahomey, Yoruba and other tribes believed in. The supreme being, the Creator, source of life, did not differentiate between Man and Woman. In a novel *Farewell to night* James Ngugi writes of a myth about the

creation and origins of the Kikuyu (Kenya): "But do you know", thus spoke father Ngotho to his son Njoroges and other peers, "that at the beginning of things there was only one man, Kikuyu, and one woman, Mubi. And God put them under a fig-tree. And at that moment the sun went up and the dark of night melted away. The sun shone with its warmth, which awoke life in all things ..." The Creator, also called Murungu, brought both Man and Woman to the place of origin of the Kikuyu: "He showed them the whole land—yes, children, God showed Kikuyu and Mubi the whole land and said to them: 'I give this land into your hands, oh man and woman. You shall rule it and bring sacrifices to the end of your days only to me, your God, under my holy fig-tree ...'"

The environment and all the actions and activities of members of the pre-class and early class-society in Africa were traditionally perceived, understood and interpreted in terms of religious beliefs. Names of people had religious significance, rocks and trees were heavy with religious symbolism and the drum spoke a religious language. Ancient traditions had a formative influence on peoples' characters and were expressed by their customs, feelings, opinions, ambitions and aspirations. The past, present and future merged into one plane and were, in a sense, experienced "simultaneously". Just as space was perceived from the perspective of the limited horizon of an agricultural, peasant society, so, too, their perception of time reflected the changing seasons and the sequence of agricultural tasks. Everything went according to the relentless rhythms imposed by nature: days, months, seasons, years; birth, marriage, procreation, death and entry into the ranks of the departed. The sun's position in the sky, milking time, times when the fields were tilled, times for the preparation and eating of meals—were all that was needed to determine the day's routine. The calm, even pace of rural life and the regularly changing seasons were the chief regulators of social existence and formed the basis of social traditions. The domestic altar with a cult object represented the ancestors, and daily sacrifices were made to them. The price paid for desecration of such an altar was death. Religious customs were preserved for centuries, despite slight changes. Particular people were endowed with magical powers: priests, nobles, in particular the king, but also "important" people such as pregnant women, mothers of twins, and virgins. All important stages in life (birth, maturity, marriage, death) but also practical activities (hunting, tilling the fields, looking after the animals, fishing, making tools, curing the sick) were connected with magic in Africa and with the belief in the magical powers of drawings scratched on stones, masks, magic herbs, incantations, dances and rituals involving stones or pieces of bone.

In West Africa and the Congo, but also in other regions earthly kings and queens were often exalted to the position of heavenly monarchs, shrouded in myths, taboos, prohibitions and superstitions, and their ancestors were declared to have been gods.

When the transition from the original, primitive religions to belief in several gods took place, the "Great Mother" lost her throne, but women as givers of life retained for a long time an important position of equal privilege which was supported by the collective consciousness of the peoples. In many parts of Africa this or that privilege or this or that particular freedom for women received frequent expression. And even in places where matrilinearity had been replaced by patrilinearity the original matrilinear organization was still discernable in myths, religious beliefs, customs and traditions (e.g. in the myths about Creation, sagas about the origins of the tribes, the Ultimate Mother, and even in the myths concerning kings). Patrilinearity received strong support from Christian and Islamic teaching. But the fact that African women managed to defend their position is supported by countless reports from earliest times right down to the Middle Ages.

Early writings relate, with some surprise, of African peoples where the dominance of women prevailed at the cost of a limitation of the rights of men. Right down to modern times women are found as regents, city founders, army commanders, officers and soldiers in female regiments or as bodyguards, with which many a king would surround himself at court. In the old kingdom of Congo women enjoyed freedom and respect. It was reported that in some tribes the birth of a girl was a cause for rejoicing, while the birth of a boy brought no such celebration. At the turn of the 17th/18th century P. Antonio Zucchelli of Gradisca reports in his travelogue *Remarkable descriptions of missions and journeys to the Congo in Ethiopia* that a Congolese bard, in a song of praise to his king, made particular mention of the fact that the king's mother was especially revered.

In West Africa, formerly the area of the Nok civilization, most of the ethnic groups retained a more or less clear organization on kinship lines right into the 19th century. Characteristic for this was the ritual head of the village community, the chief. The patrilinear system predominated, but in some groups the matrilinear system had been retained. In others there was a bilateral system (mother's and father's line), and even today a number of major ethnic groups in the western Sudan has retained this. P. Rattray did, however, point out that in more modern times the freedom and independence of women in ethno-social units in which the patrilinear system is not fully established, does have its limits. Using the example of Ashanti women, he establishes that the freedom of women "was almost entirely dependent on their virtually complete subordination to the other family linked by blood with the husband." (124) One final interesting example from the south of Africa can be given: In southern and southeastern Africa the famous nineteenth-century British missionary and traveller David Livingstone came across a tribe living on the Zambesi in which women had the same legal status as men. They sat among the tribal elders and their authority was respected in the family. The husband usually took the woman's village as his chief place of residence. In doing so he committed himself to care for his mother in perpetuity. In the case of separation the man returned to his village, but left the children behind in the mother's village. The woman was head of the household and was committed to feed the husband and children. In his observations of family disputes, Livingstone observed that women often employed an extremely effective weapon to punish their undiscerning husbands—starvation.

There is much evidence to suggest that the transition to a patrilinear system of organization of the relations between men and women involved a number of stages. Elements of matrilinear organization persisted for a long time. Social values—religion, customs and traditions—meant that a sudden transition was not possible. In some regions, among some peoples and tribes, the social inequality between the sexes and the exploitation of women's work increased, but in other places this or that privilege for women persisted doggedly. Old traditions remained despite the increasing division of labour.

For some people the clinging to old customs and social values proved to be an inhibiting factor, for others a welcome protection, a possibility to adapt to new conditions—both existed parallel to each other. Every individual in ancient Africa led an existence which bore a deep imprint of religion, from birth to death. One's entire existence was a religious event, man was a religious being in a religious universe. Marriage and the family were religious processes, whether it was traditional ancestor-worship, fetishism, the belief in several gods, or in the case of Christianity and Islam a monotheistic faith which determined people's lives. Life followed the traditional rituals, and the daily routine was thus embued with meaning and validity.

Concealed behind ideological considerations, which should not be underestimated, there were, in the last analysis, socio-economic factors. One significant reason why matrilinearity continued to exert an influence on the position of women for a very long time was the absolute predominance of the rural population. Agriculture constituted the economic basis for most peo-ple, either crop-growing or animal husbandry or both together. These were supplemented by hunting, gathering and fishing (which, in the case of peoples such as the bushmen, pygmies and other primitive communities are still the main form of economic activity). Specialized activities such as craftwork, trading etc. were integrated into economies dominated by animal husbandry and agriculture. In tropical regions women played a predominant role in agriculture, tilling the soil with digging stick or hoe and cultivating tuber or root crops. Their role here was much greater than in animal husbandry, and this remained the case for centuries. This underlines the significance of the original, natural division of labour between the sexes, which gave rise to the social division of labour. This early situation had a decisive influence on the development of relations between the sexes. In tribes in which agriculture predominated, matrilinearity persisted, whereas in those raising animals, the development was more in a patrilinear direction.

Women also played an important role in the life of the family and the village community. They helped feed the family, very often being the chief providers of nourishment, they bore and brought up children; and they often retained an especially respected position within the extended family. In rural communities the dividing line between domestic work and socially productive work was not a clear one. For a long time the role and function of women in ancient Africa proved to be an inhibiting influence (depending on the region concerned) on the general law, discernible throughout the world, whereby the emergence of private property led to the increasing economic and legal dependence of women on men within marriage.

The individual tasks involved in work in the fields were divided up between men and women and many of these have to this day remained the prerogative of women. Even in tribes where animal husbandry, tilling the fields, craftwork and trade—in other words, a division of labour—were highly developed, a system of equal rights persisted for a long period. One important and long-lasting influence on the relationship between the matrilinear and the patrilinear principles was Islam. Islam penetrated further into Africa than did Christianity, and can to this day be seen to have had a detrimental influence on the social status of women. Many peoples in eastern, central and western Africa adopted the Islamic faith. It spread through the areas south of the Sahara, which shared similar historical development and social differentiation, and a wide-ranging exchange of cultural values took place. Islam took on elements of the traditional African religious beliefs and adapted partially to local social conditions. The spread of Islam along the eastern coast of Africa took place at roughly the same time as its spread into Arabia. The colony of Kilwa, founded in the 10th century, became an important centre of Islam, followed by Mombasa, Zanzibar, Mozambique, Sofala and dozens of other city states. The new religion spread into the area between the lakes of central Africa. It penetrated the island territory of Madagascar. Conversion of the east and southeastern coasts was complete by the 18th century, with the exception of Ethiopia, Madagascar and one or two areas of limited size, such as southern Sudan. In West Africa, Is-

19

Gold weights which were used for weighing gold dust with tiny hand scales. These weights, from the area which is today Ghana, often bore depictions of scenes from everyday life which give clues as to the legal status of women. Museum für Völkerkunde, Leipzig.

lam started to spread from the 8th century onwards. Arab trading caravans crossing from north to western Africa by the ancient trading routes, brought the new religion to the states beyond the Sahara. At the end of the 11th century the conquering of Ghana by the Almoravides, members of an Islamic movement among the Berber tribes, marked the beginning of the spread of the faith in West Africa. It spread to the old territories of Mali, Songhai and Kanem-Bornu, the Hausa states in what is now northern Nigeria, the Yoruba territories and Benin.

The influence of Islam often seems to have persisted only in superficial, external characteristics, such as clothing, jewellery, eating customs, some rituals and traditions etc. Even when Islam obtained a stronger footing, for example in the cities, many aspects of traditional African life and ways of thinking survived. Many ethical and family values which emerged with early patrilinear class developments were close to Islamic beliefs or at least had certain points in common with them (e.g. polygamy) and were accepted by the followers of the new religion. However, the Koran, the basis for Islam, had a negative effect on the life of women because it lent an aura of sanctity to the patrilinear traditions which had little or no support from the traditional religious beliefs. Islam strengthened the power and authority of the ruling dynasties and the emerging early-feudal aristocracy. The Islamic ruling classes used the religious element to create a system of exploitation in which women constituted a particularly oppressed group.

It should be noted, however, that village communities and traditional social institutions in rural areas remained largely untouched by the new religion right into the 16th century. Thus Ibn Battuta, in his description of a journey to Mali reports: "Wives display no modesty in form of men and do not wear veils, although they take an active part in prayers ..."

Among many of the agricultural peoples it was possible to observe a retention of the old African tradition of equality of the sexes. Abbé Demanet, in his book *Modern history of French Africa*, written towards the end of the 18th century, writes about his observations of the practical attitude of Islam towards the female sex: "Despite the fact that Mahomet excluded women both from the necessity of circumcision and from paradise, there are benign teachers who concede a tiny corner of paradise to women on condition that they allow themselves to be circumcised—inasmuch as this is possible for their sex. In all places where this doctrine, which is advantageous to the other sex, has been accepted, female circumcision is carried out." (20)

Other accounts confirm this "correction" to Islamic teaching in West Africa. Thus Paul Jacob Bruns reports: "It is well known that, according to the Koran, women are not circumcised and therefore have to do without entry to paradise. But because the Mandingo do not exclude women from paradise, they also allow them to be circumcised, but by other women." (26)

In rural areas the old matrilinear elements proved to be stronger, even among nomadic shepherds. Thus the common law prevailing among many nomadic tribes in the Sahara shows very clear traces of matrilinear elements. An example of this is the Tuaregs, who, although embracing Islamic beliefs, were strictly monogamous. A wife was a lifelong partner of the man, and possessed equal rights. She controlled and administered the common possessions, while the man concerned himself with relationships with other tribes, with warring and with hunting. According to the ethnographer P. Fuchs, among the Tuaregs it was not the women but the men who covered their faces. The woman "frequently has the last word in family matters. And in many respects the position of the child in the family is determined by the authority of the woman. Children do not inherit according to the male line but according to the female line, especially that of the wife's oldest brother, who largely determines the fate of the child." Tuareg women accompanied their husbands on hunting trips, handled the camels and horses with equal skill and even took part in forays and battles.

Such a complex interweaving of patrilinear and matrilinear elements cannot have come about merely by chance. An explanation can be found in socio-economic conditions. Some of the Tuaregs maintained for a long time the nomadic way of life raising camels, sheep and goats. But many nomads combined animal husbandry with crop-growing, and women played a dominant role in the cultivation of millet, wheat, beans and vegetables. European travellers discovered, each in his own way, that, regardless of whether or not Islamic beliefs prevailed, in various, mainly rural African tribes relations between the sexes were characterized by a degree of equality unusual for Islamic communities.

Queens, princesses, court ladies and Amazons

In many African countries the inhabitants retained memories of famous female rulers and warriors, co-regents and queen mothers.

On the following pages some of the women are mentioned from the great number of female rulers who went down in the history of their country or were indeed famous beyond its borders.

In Ethiopia, the oldest state in Africa for which records exist, the state dates back three thousand years B.C., matriarchy was strong in pre-Christian times. Around 1000 B.C. the Napata Empire was founded, later to be called Meroe. In the year 22 B.C. this area was conquered by the Romans. As the Roman historian Strabo reported, the leader of the African army was Queen Kandake, who tried in vain to resist the Roman troops under Augustus Caesar.

In the tenth century A.D., when the Ethiopian Empire of Aksum was beginning to crumble, the story goes that Queen Judith and her troops rose against the kings of Aksum, destroyed the city, overturned the obelisks, and took over complete control. It was not until orthodox Christianity arrived in the 4th century A.D., first in the north of the country, and then spread throughout the country by 1500, that the claim to power of men won through—but then only after a long period of development.

One of the oldest and most powerful of the kingdoms of Arabia was Sheba, from where countless trading states on the Red Sea coast were established, in the area today known as Eritrea. This was, according to the Bible and the Koran, the sphere of influence of the "Queen of Sheba". She became a mythical co-founder of the Christian kingdom. Her liaison with King Solomon gave rise to the first king of the Solomonide dynasty, which ruled this north-east African region from 1270 onwards. The new "state mythology", based on the Old Testament, was also linked with the traditional African kingdom and with remains of matrilinearity. According to this late Christian legend, the Queen of Sheba was Ethiopian.

In the Sudanese state of Wadai, founded in 1650 under Islamic influence, the Queen Mother, the Magira, had considerable influence on politics. This state was much feared on account of its excellent army which it possessed from 1800 onwards.

West Africa offers a particularly interesting example for matrilinearity and its influence. In the first half of the 15th century Queen Amina ruled the kingdom of the Songhai in mid-Niger. Oral accounts relate of the life and deeds of this ruler who was a famous warrior and waged successful campaigns against neighbouring territories, extending her empire as far as the Atlantic coast. She founded cities, received tributes from mighty tribal chiefs, and is reputed to have introduced the cola nut to this part of Africa.

In one of their songs the Ashanti sang about the ruler Guebi Saa Ababoi Wankii, who was renowned for the generosity and understanding which she displayed towards the suffering and neediness of the simple people. If a family needed help because of fire, crop failure, illness or death, this was given to them.

The British ethnographer F. Meyerowitz identified in the folk-tales of the Akan (Ghana) the names of many co-regents. In one of the Ashanti states eighteen queens were reputed to have reigned between 1295 and 1740. From time to time they undertook journeys through the villages, met their subjects and, where necessary, came to their aid.

In West Africa it was the coast of Senegal which European travellers first got to know. The French traveller, Abbé Demanet, in his *Modern history of French Africa* reported about the high status of women at the royal courts. When diplomatic negotiations were being carried out with foreigners, the king was always surrounded by his wives, whom he introduced like all his court grandees. "His Favourite sits on a seat beside him, his prime minister is on his left, and the foreigner also sits in a chair, opposite the king. The grandees of the court sit on mats and form the first circle, in the centre of which the foreigner sits with his interpreters, who, however, have to remain standing. The second circle contains the king's other wives, who also stand; in the third circle come the more important officers." At religious ceremonies, too, women had places of honour. The custom also existed of his wives joining their husband in the grave when a king died—not just those whom he had particularly loved, but also those who were necessary "to serve his every pleasure in the other world".

Other travellers in West Africa in the 17th and 18th centuries were also struck by the privileged position of women at royal courts. Of the Wolof, a negroid people of the West Bantu language group belonging to the Senegalese peoples, who had lived on the coast of Senegal since 1446, it was said that the kings surrounded themselves with countless ladies of the court, including some who were married to them. One of these had apparently equal status with the king. Theophil Friedrich Ehrmann reports: "The queen had ... visited the white stranger; now the other wives of the king also wished to see him, so he was led into the courtyard of their building; they immediately sprang out of their huts, surrounded him and filled the air with piercing screams and astonished laughter ... All

of them displayed much surprise and curiosity. They plied him with questions about where he came from, the colour of his skin, about white women, their attitude towards love, about their husbands and their behaviour towards women." (27) In *Historical and Philosophical Sketches of the Discoveries and Settlements of the Europeans in North and West Africa at the End of the Eighteenth Century*, which Carl Steudel translated into German, one can read the following about the Wolof: "In some of these states the head of state is elected, in others the position is hereditary. As the negroes can be more certain who the mother of a specific child is than who the father is, the line of inheritance goes across to the male line on the female side; thus, instead of the elder son of the king inheriting his father's position, it is passed on from the eldest son to the king's eldest sister." (32)

Mothers enjoyed great respect. In particular the mother of the king often played an important role. It was not necessary for her to be the actual mother or wife of a king, for the title "Queen Mother" was largely honorary. In ancient Africa unmarried princesses were customarily called "Queen Mother" if their lineage was so exalted that they were forbidden to marry. They were nevertheless allowed to have illegitimate children, from whose ranks then later the future pretenders to the throne were chosen. Thus a princess could also become queen mother. Usually the queen mother possessed extensive amounts of land, and a personal court, and she often had the final word in important state affairs. Thus it was reported from Monomotapa that women had important positions at the court of the king. The queen mother was respected as the "mother of all kings" and wielded considerable power. She had her own court and her voice carried much weight in the king's council.

A further example for the role of the queen mother was to be found in the Zulu Empire which developed at the beginning of the 1820s in the densely populated southeastern part of Africa and extended from the Limpopo to the edge of the Cape. It was said of the

20

The figure "ibeji" is the god of twins. If a twin dies, the mother orders two figures from an artist. As the Yoruba believe that the soul of twins is indivisible, the dead child lives on in the wooden figure and takes part in the life of the other twin. This figure is also washed, oiled, fed, dressed etc. Ibeji figure. Height 30 cm. Yoruba, Nigeria. Museum für Völkerkunde, Frankfurt/ Main.

21

Recognition of African woman as "Creator" was one of the original ideas of traditional religions. The Senufo, for example, worshipped this mother goddess. Ritual statue of the Senufo. Rietbergmuseum, Zurich.

Stylized female sculptures. Height 22–23 cm. Bagirmi. Museum für Völkerkunde, Frankfurt/ Main.

23

Queen Mother. Setting for an ivory tooth for the worship of royal ancestors. Cast bronze. 18th–19th century. Height 56 cm. Benin, Nigeria. Museum für Völkerkunde, Dresden.

24

The art of woodcarving was largely a matter for the men. If a carver was working on sacred figures or masks connected with ancestor-worship or magic, women and children were not alldrowed to watch him at work. The artist emphasized certain elements, schematized some and often omitted details. Ancestral figure. Height 46.5 cm. Northern Bakuba, Eastern Congo. Rietbergmuseum, Zurich.

25

In the courtly art of medieval Benin, there are many representations of queens and princesses. Queen Mother. Bronze. Height 51 cm. Benin, Nigeria. Museum für Völkerkunde, Staatliche Museen Preussischer Kulturbesitz, Berlin (West).

26

Representation of a queen. Brass. Height 21 cm. Benin, Nigeria. Museum für Völkerkunde, Staatliche Museen Preussischer Kulturbesitz, Berlin (West).

27

Wooden mask of the Wamuera/Makonde. Woman with facial tattoos and lip-disc, around 1910. Height 21.5 cm, width 14 cm. Museum für Völkerkunde, Dresden.

28

These sculptured heads
originally stood on the
ancestors' altars of the
royal family and were
used for religious rituals.
The bronzes were created
by craftsmen working
exclusively for the king.
The frieze is decorated
with animal figures.
Bronze. Height 31.5 cm.
Benin, Nigeria. Museum
für Völkerkunde, Leipzig.

29

The first European trav-
ellers often reported
in some awe about the
rights and freedoms
enjoyed by women and
about the privileges
enjoyed by the king's
daughters. Princess
Edeleyo. Brass. Height
46.5 cm. Benin, Nigeria.
Museum für Völker-
kunde, Staatliche Museen
Preussischer Kulturbesitz,
Berlin (West).

30

Ancestor-worship played
a preeminent role. Fig-
ures of ancestors such as
this pair belonging to the
Dogon had a privileged
place in the family and
tribal organization of the
peasants. Depiction of
a pair of grandparents.
Mali. Rietbergmuseum,
Zurich.

31

Right up to the present
day the tradition of town
markets has remained
unchanged. The market
is the scene of trading,
bargaining and exchange
of news. Kenya.

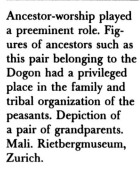

32

The privileged position of women in old Africa resulted in a variety of artistic subjects. This equestrian figure was a hunting fetish supposed to bring luck to the hunters. Made in one piece, blackened surface. Height 40 cm. Village of Latka, Ivory Coast. Staatliches Museum für Völkerkunde, Linden-Museum, Stuttgart.

Wooden chief's stool,
depicting a woman with
scar-tattooing. Early
20th century. Height
46.5 cm. Zaïre, Luba
region. Museum für
Völkerkunde, Dresden.

Woman with basket.
Bronze cast, around
1900. Height 15.5 cm.
Gold Coast (Ghana),
Ashanti. Museum für
Völkerkunde, Dresden.

35

This stool is one of countless artistically created objects which have been preserved up till the present day. Grasslands of the Cameroon. Wood, partly blackened. Height 36.5 cm. Diameter 38 cm. Museum für Völkerkunde, Leipzig.

36

Court artists created impressive depictions of the privileged position of mother of the ruler, who was himself worshipped virtually as a god. High-ranking individuals are differentiated from their servants by size. Queen with followers. Benin, Nigeria. Rautenstrauch-Joest-Museum, Cologne.

37

Idols were preservers of
life energy and mediators
between the living and
the world of gods and
spirits. The particular criteria of beauty and pro-
portions were the result
of the beliefs and rituals
of the individual tribes.

Idol. Height 32 cm.
Teke, Central Africa.
Staatliches Museum für
Völkerkunde, Linden-
Museum, Stuttgart.

Mothers were shown
particular social respect,
and various depictions
of them were created.
Mother with child. Sculp-
ture. Height 56 cm.
Dogon, West Africa.
Staatliches Museum für
Völkerkunde, Linden-
Museum, Stuttgart.

39

Masks such as this were worn by secret societies which served to preserve old traditions and defend them against new influences. Mask. Cross River region, Nigeria. Height 29.5 cm. Museum für Völkerkunde, Leipzig.

40

At an early stage, women established their position in urban markets and in trade in general. Market group in Bamum, Cameroon, in the 19th century.

41

As late as 1900 privileged women demonstrated their status by their clothing, jewellery and other symbols. The Queen Mother Njabudunke with litter and followers. Bamum, Cameroon.

42/43

Women of the various tribes wear characteristic hairstyles and fertility symbols. The wife of a king from Cameroon also bears tattoo decorations and the young Bamum woman has the traditional pigtails.

44

The lifestyle and clothing of the population between the Gold Coast and the Niger delta are depicted on a historical map of Africa from the year 1743 according to the reports of contemporary travellers. Sächsische Landesbibliothek, Dresden.

talented king and army commander Chaka (1787 to 1828) who led the much-feared Zulu warriors, that later the mere mention of his name was enough to strike terror into the hearts of the people.

Legend has it that Chaka sacrificed 1,000 cattle on the death of his mother, ten virgins were chosen to be buried alive with the body of the departed, and his warriors waged countless campaigns in honour of the dead queen mother.

Often the king and queen mother reigned together—sometimes with the wife or sister of the king. At tribal and family level too there was in many cases a sharing of power between male and female chiefs. The female chief had main responsibility for women's affairs.

In a number of West African states a government was formed by the elected king, his sister, the queen mother, and a council of elders. Often the succession passed from the eldest sister of the king. The role of the queen mother, marriage of sisters, and the ritual murder of the king, common in many African countries, all have their roots in matriarchal traditions.

In the 17th and 18th centuries countless travellers reported that African princesses enjoyed positions of privilege. No man was allowed to refuse their wishes. More recently, however, writers have questioned the existence of polyandry, the marriage of one woman with several men, which was said to prevail among rulers. In his *History of Loango, Kakongo and other kingdoms of Africa* the French Abbé Proyart reports on the privileges of these people: "A princess possesses the double right to select a husband of her choice from among her subjects and to force him to have no other wife than herself. Because this last condition strikes the princes as being too harsh, there are few among them who desire to marry a princess... They furthermore have the right—unlike most wives—to separate from a man who does not please them and to select another." (19)

Among the Herero in South-West Africa (Namibia) the daughter of a chief had a special position. She had the task of tending the sacred fire in her hut and, at dusk, to mark the beginning of milking time—the Herero were largely cattle-rearers—she brought the fire out into the open.

Interesting details of the role of women within the state can be gleaned from areas of the Congo region, where female regents or co-regents could be found—queens, queen mothers and female chiefs. P. Antonio Zucchelli wrote at the beginning of the 18th century about the "ruling queen, Donna Veronica" (a name given to her by the mission) and about a princess whom he named "Donna Susanne di Nobrena, a daughter, sister and mother of three kings who ruled the Congo one after the other, who was ninety years of age and was hardly able to see any more."

When the female co-regent of Sogno died, ten thousand warriors "all armed with bow and arrows" appeared at the funeral ceremony. The noble lady was buried with full honours, sumptuously clothed and bejewelled. For several months all celebrations were banned and "trumpets and drums" were silent. (15)

In the Lunda kingdom in the Congo there was, beside the king, who was called Mwata Yamvo, a queen, the Lukokesha, who was not the wife of the ruler but just a member of the royal house. She had her own court, income and—most importantly—played a decisive role in the election of the king. She was allowed to marry, and her husbands were classified officially as women and possessed no power whatsoever. The Lukokesha was always the daughter of a Mwata Yamvo and received the income from several provinces. She wore, as a sign of her position, an arm-ring and rich jewellery on her bosom.

After the disintegration of the old Congo kingdom one of the most powerful states in the Congo basin was Ndongo, called Angola by the Portuguese because it was ruled by the Ngola dynasty. In 1622 a delegation from this royal family appeared before the Portuguese viceroy in Luanda. At their head was an unusual woman, the African princess Nzinga Mbande Ngola. She came on the request of her brother, king Ngola

Mbande, accompanied by a substantial retinue and invested with considerable powers. Her task was to negotiate with the Portuguese about the peace treaty which the latter had offered.

In honour of the occasion, the viceroy arranged for a cannon salute to be fired as would occur on the occasion of such a state visit in Europe. But at the same time he had made sure that during the audience he would be the real master and the princess would appear as his subject. He wished to express this fact by the seating order he arranged for the negotiation sessions. Thus, in the reception room a velvet seat decorated with gold, intended for the governor, had pride of place. Opposite it there lay a priceless carpet with piles of velvet cushions. On entering the room Nzinga Mbande Ngola summed up the situation at a glance. Without batting an eyelid or saying a word—so the capuchin missionary Cavazzi reports—she signalled with a glance to one of her ladies-in-waiting for the latter to kneel down and offer her back to the princess. She sat down on this, as on a seat, and remained in this position for the rest of the audience. As the chronicler reported, this incident caused something of a sensation among the Portuguese, which was increased by the diplomatic skills displayed by the princess, her cleverness and the dignity with which she behaved. She demanded an honourable peace and made it clear that this would be to the advantage of both sides. She amazed and utterly convinced the council, devastating them with the logic of her arguments that the most senior officials and council members were incapable of countering any of them effectively.

Nzinga Mbande Ngola was born in 1582, shortly after the Portuguese Paolo Diaz occupied a small area of Angola with his expedition. The Angolans, armed with lances, axes and knives, resisted, and King Ngola Mbande succeeded, in 1620, in preventing the invaders from penetrating the interior of the country. A breathing-space was regarded as necessary, and this was the reason why the king had sent the princess on a diplomatic mission to Luanda in 1622.

The governor wished to form an alliance with the proud, unyielding princess. He called up learned men to teach her the sacraments of Christian belief, and Nzinga was baptized, at the age of 40, in the cathedral in Luanda. The governor and his wife, Donna Anna, attended the ceremony, and the wife's name was given to the new convert as a Christian name.

Nzinga Mbande Ngola was 42 when her brother died and she succeeded to the throne in 1624. In the same year she left the Christian faith, partly under pressure from her courtiers among whom the opinion was being expressed that "the king should not so easily give up the religion of his ancestors because he would thus be bowing to a foreign law", and partly as a deliberate gesture of opposition to the Portuguese. She took up the fight against the Portuguese once again, and waged many successful campaigns right up to the middle of the 17th century. As a result she is often referred to in the literature as a sort of African Joan of Arc.

Nzinga's court displayed unusual splendour, and Cavazzi assures us that it contained as many courtiers as European counterparts. One particularly important ceremony was the queen's midday meal. She usually sat on a raffia mat to eat and took the food by hand out of the dishes. But towards the end of her life she increasingly ate in the European style, sitting at a table on which there were silver plates. During the meal she conversed with the ladies of the court and her confidantes and she used to hand them pieces of meat "which they accepted with much reverence". Cavazzi tells us that he once counted as many as 60 courses. During the meals Nzinga asked her courtiers questions "which displayed the sharpness of her mind". As the queen, according to Cavazzi, had many spies who told her about everything that was going on, she often astonished those around her, who were convinced that she was able to penetrate into the innermost secrets of their hearts.

In contrast to the royal courts of Europe, the highest positions at Nzinga's court were taken by women.

Cavazzi tells us that Nzinga followed tradition in filling every position with a man and a woman. The women in the queen's retinue displayed military skills, strength and bravery, they learned to use weapons and went to war, like Amazons, with the queen.

Some sources report that custom did not allow a woman to be the absolute ruler. Nzinga solved this in an interesting manner: she wore a man's clothing and her retinue consisted of several youths who wore the apparel of concubines. Cavazzi reports, however, that she was waited on by 300 women. There was also a council, which exercised the task of ruling the country and served as the highest military and religious organ, as well as being the ultimate legal body. Many legal matters were, however, decided on by Nzinga herself. She punished people of simple origins often with harsh sentences; for relatively harmless crimes she would have their throats slit or would have them thrown to wild animals. In the case of crimes committed by people of higher status, such punishments were less common. A Netherlandish officer described her as "a crafty, proud and stubborn woman, who was so fascinated by weapons that she hardly had time for anything else; furthermore she never did harm to a Portuguese if he had been pardoned ..." (13)

Nzinga Mbande Ngola allied with the Netherlands against the Portuguese in 1641 and skilfully exploited the rivalry between the two colonial powers. In 1656 the elderly queen once again had to sign a compromise peace treaty with the Portuguese. One of the reasons was the fact that the Portuguese were resorting to the measure of installing puppet kings in parts of Nzinga's territory. In April 1657 the peace treaty was signed. As a condition of her and her followers being baptized again in church she insisted that her sister, who had been in captivity for many years, should be released. The governor agreed to this, provided Nzinga delivered 200 slaves to him. Queen Nzinga died on the 17th December 1663 at the age of 81. She had combined in her person the roles of statesman, army commander and diplomat.

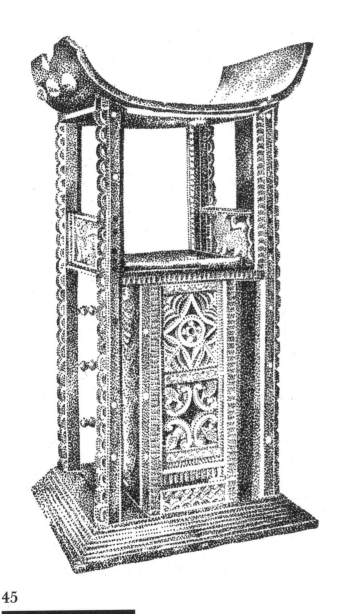

45

Wood-working in West Africa, with its long traditions, depicts the power and greatness of the kings in countless ways. Throne of Gléle, king of Dahomey (1858–89). Musée de l'Homme, Paris.

A more recent example of a woman playing a role in the highest offices of state can be found on the island of Madagascar. The influence of old African monarchical systems extended even to this island, which was ruled by a succession of queens: Ranavalona I, Rasoaherina, Ranavalona II, and Ranavalona III.

The close links which Madagascar had not only with the African mainland but also with the distant islands which today form Indonesia can be seen in the language and culture of the Madagascans. The women of the island were renowned for their beauty, their fidelity and a number of other virtues. In volume 14 of the *Collection of the Best Descriptions of Voyages*, 1765, one reads: "Women can be found on this island who are far superior in courage and virtue to others of their sex. The historians of the island refer to one Dian-Rhea, who brought the entire island under her sceptre. Dian-Nong Amboulle's princess gave countless proofs of her bravery and magnanimity. Several times she went to war at his side and saved his life more than once."

By the end of the 18th century the upper classes, the Hova, had succeeded in extending their sphere of domination from the mountainous centre to the entire island. "Hova" was the name originally given to the Merina, the largest ethnic group on the island, but soon the name became extended to cover not just the independent farmers but the whole ethnic group. From that point onwards there was a structured state, a monarchy with a feudal social structure. At the head of the Madagascan state were queens, who were supported in their task of ruling the state by prime ministers who were also their husbands. Prime Minister Rainilaiarivony took over the position in 1863, and married several pretenders to the throne one after the other. The strong rivalry between Britain and France for control of the island cast a shadow over this kingdom, which had embraced the Christian faith under Prime Minister Rainilaiarivony and made it the established state religion.

In 1894 France started another colonial war over Madagascar. Madagascan resistance rallied behind the young Queen Ranavalona III (1883–1897), who was Rainilaiarivony's last wife, but resistance continued even after the royal house had capitulated. In 1897 the bloody struggle ended with the establishment of the French colonial regime. Contemporaries describe how, in February 1897, General Gallieni, the leader of the French expeditionary force, marched in full dress uniform and with drawn sword up the steps of the royal palace and ordered his soldiers to send into exile a proud, beautiful woman with sparkling black eyes set in a dusky face—Queen Ranavalona III. The castle of the Madagascan kings, the "silver palace", with the symbol of the royal family, the Voromahery, the hawk rampant, still can be seen perched high above Antanarivo—a memorial to the old Christian kingdom.

Doubtless the queens and co-regents who have been mentioned here all represented very different historical, regional and social conditions, but it is neverthe-

46

The fabled Queen Nzinga Mbande proves her dignity in negotiations with Portuguese invaders. After an old print.

less possible to make certain generalizations. Matrilinearity and matriarchy do not necessarily go together, but women as the holders of secular or religious offices do point to conditions which were characterized originally by matrilinearity. "Female kings" and armies of women (Amazons) in systems which were otherwise patrilinear are often transitional forms which mark the passing of a matrilinear system. Such transitional forms—relatively isolated pointers to former times—ensured the continued existence of special rights for individual groups of women within certain peoples for many centuries.

Old accounts of voyages make occasional reference to Amazons, female army commanders and regiments consisting of women.

In Greek myth the Amazons were a warlike group of women in Asia Minor who only tolerated men in order to ensure continuation of the race. Their favourite pastimes were said to be hunting and waging war. Their name was said to mean "breastless", because at an early age one, or even as Diodorus Siculus reported, both breasts, were removed in order that they were able to move their arms more freely and more vigorously.

In the *Iliad* Homer has old Priam tell how as a young man he and his troops once fought against "amazon man-women" in Phrygia. Herodotus also writes of Amazons whom the Hellenes defeated in the battle on the Thermodon and "then loaded all those still living on to three vehicles and sailed away." Of marriage for them it was said that "no maiden enters a marriage before she has killed an enemy; thus many die at a great age before marriage, because they are unable to fulfill the law." Herodotus says nothing about their children and their upbringing. Strabo changed the seat of the Amazons to the foot of the Caucasus and said: "All of them have their right breast burnt off when they are young, so that they can use their arm for all purposes, especially using a sling. They also have arrows, fighting axes and shields. They make headdresses, clothing and belts from animal skins." In the spring it was said that they got together with other peoples "for the sake of producing offspring". Male offspring was sent to the father, females were retained and brought up by the women themselves.

If one reduces the Greek sagas to their essence what remains is the fact that in ancient times there existed tribes which contained independent armed groups of women who did not marry but did occasionally have relationships with men. The historical basis for sagas about the Amazons was presumably matrilinear tribes in declining primitive society. Another interpretation was that the daughter of a father who had no son could be brought up as a son, would behave like a man and would learn to use weapons.

There is a particularly valuable reference to be found in Diodorus Siculus in which he describes the African Amazons. "In the western parts of Libya, at the frontiers of the world, there is supposed to have been a nation ruled by women; they waged war, served for a defined period in the army during which period they had to exist without men. When their years of service were past, they get together with men in order to perpetuate their race. Public office and general administration are, however, retained as their exclusive domain. Men live domestic lives like women in our society, and obey the orders of their spouses; they play no role in war, government and other matters of state, as such activities might make them rebel against their wives. Straight after birth, male offspring is handed over to the father, who feeds him with milk and other foods according to his age. If the child is female, however, her breasts are burned so that they do not grow in puberty, for it is regarded as an encumbrance for the carrying of weapons if the breasts project from the body; for this reason they are called Amazons (breastless) by the Greeks." Accounts indulged in a certain amount of exaggeration, and it is likely that even the burning off of breasts was a misunderstanding, even though it may have been the case that growth of the breasts was discouraged by any external means.

Archaeological evidence suggests that Amazons existed in early times in Africa. The French researcher, Henri Lhote, who started to examine the rock drawings of the Sahara at the beginning of the 1930s and again at the beginning of the 1950s, discovered the so-called "Fresco of the twelve steps" at Sefar. In addition to mouflons, elephants, giraffes and other animals, the drawings depict a battle scene in which—to the surprise of the onlooker—the bow-carrying warriors turn out to be women.

Magrizi, the medieval Arab writer, described how the women among the African Beja tribe made lances at a spot which no men were allowed to live at or to visit, except when they wanted to buy a weapon. Basically the Amazons were nothing more than a female grouping which usually existed within their tribe and probably only seldom lived separately from it.

In medieval Europe there was a rumour that the sources of the Nile were guarded by a fierce tribe of Amazons. Old travellers' reports also provide interesting accounts, even though they should be approached with a certain degree of caution, as such European travellers often allowed themselves to be influenced by their memories of Greek myths. Again and again, women are mentioned who served as bodyguards for African rulers.

One report was given by Eduard López, who visited the kingdom of Monomotapa in central Africa. Here there were women serving the ruler who were renowned for their skill in using bows and arrows. They lived in an area given them as a fief by the ruler and were occasionally visited by the men for intercourse. According to a later report, the Sultan of Sokoto had at his court in the 19th century a large group of female singers who accompanied him everywhere wearing bright clothes on horseback, and were forbidden to enter into legal marriages.

Even at the end of the 19th century Dahomey (Benin, West Africa today) had regiments of Amazons. Since the 17th century this kingdom, founded by the Ewe, had had the name of Dahomey. The king

47

Amazons, as seen through the eyes of European travellers. From: *General History of Voyages by Land and Sea …*, Leipzig 1747. Forschungsbibliothek Gotha.

The Legal Situation

was an absolute monarch. His orders were carried out by a ministry which in 1800 consisted of three ministers, one for trade and military affairs, one for police and justice, and a minister for the Royal Household.

The royal palace was in the capital, Abomey, which was about a three days' journey away from the port of Wydah, on the coast. In the 19th century the town had about 24,000 inhabitants. The king's palace was an enormous, extensive affair surrounded by several high mud walls. Around the palace itself were countless buildings separated by courtyards. Emissaries and other important visitors were received by the king in a large hall decorated with reliefs depicting the most important events in the history of the kingdom.

The Amazons guarded the king's palace and took part in many battles. They wore uniforms, were well armed, seasoned warriors and famous for their discipline and courage. The Amazon guard was said to have consisted originally of 5,000 girls and to have been first formed in 1729. Sources conflict on this point. Since 1835 their quarters round the king's palace had formed a separate township which, by the end of the century had almost 8,000—exclusively female—inhabitants.

The Amazons in Dahomey were different from others in that they were not permitted to have contacts with men, at least as long as they bore arms. They were compelled to be chaste. Once their military service was over they were allowed to marry. Precisely because the Amazons of Dahomey played an important role right up to the end of the 19th century it is interesting to have a lively portrayal of their activities. In the *Description of Nigritia*, 1765, from the pen of a "Mr. P, former member of the high council in Senegal and commandant of Fort St. Louis", one can read that the king's palace was only guarded by women, the monarch only received visitors in the presence of "five or six women who sat on a carpet" and only his women were allowed to break the taboo against observing the monarch, who claimed divine origin, while

at table. On special occasions the much-described parades of troops took place, in which regiments of women played a prominent role. The French author describes how the royal household guard paraded on the occasion of the audience which he had with the king: "At this point there emerges from a large courtyard the female warriors of the king, which consists of small units of eighty to one hundred well-armed women, each carrying a small musket and a little short sword whose scabbard is usually made of crimson velvet. Their clothing consists of nothing more than a small silk cloth round their loins which hangs down to their knees. Armed in this way and carrying two or three banners, these women march in ranks four-deep slowly into the courtyard where the king's shaded throne is and greet him three times with their banners. After one or two circuits the first unit retires, to be replaced immediately by another, similarly armed, and then three or four more, whose leaders are awarded gifts by the king if their manoeuvres have pleased him. All the women in these units are little more than sixteen or seventeen years old, with the exception of their leaders, who are older." (24) Another report written by the Englishman, John Duncan, on Dahomey, contains a description of the king's bodyguard about a hundred years later. These regiments are by now also led by men; one of them belongs to "a son of the king, the governor of one of the provinces", and another to the king's second son.

"The speed of these women, despite the fact that they are carrying a long Danish musket, a short sword and a sort of club, would astonish a European." The women's weapons and clothing have changed by the time this report was written: "They wear a blue and white striped armless undergarment made of coarse, locally woven cotton, which allows them to move their arms freely. The lower part of the dress is the length of a Scottish highlander's kilt, and the short trousers worn underneath reach down to two inches below their knees. The cartridge-holder or 'agbwadya' is in the form of a belt which holds the clothing together securely. It contains twenty cartridges. The powder, which is carried in a leather capsule, is poured into the muzzle of the musket without using a plug, and as the balls are also slid loosely into the barrel, the shot, which anyhow is loosed off more or less at random rather than being aimed at a specific target, naturally looses a lot of its force. Generally speaking, however, these female warriors are an extremely impressive sight. The women are very agile, and, thanks to the constant exercise which they have here and elsewhere, including their work in the home and in the fields, can withstand considerable physical stress." (42) John Duncan writes that he had often heard these female warriors of the king of Dahomey mentioned by others, but that now he had also seen for himself these "well-armed, usually beautiful, strong and healthy women". He describes a military exercise which involved the storming of a settlement protected by a stockade made of thorns. Impressed by what he saw, Duncan wrote that if he were to undertake a military campaign "I would prefer these female warriors to the male ones of this country. One of the female officers of the king's corps, who I was introduced to, was called Adadimo. In each of the last two annual military campaigns she had taken a male prisoner, and the king had rewarded her with promotion and the present of two female slaves. Adadimo is a tall, slim woman, quite pretty as blacks go, about twenty-two years old and of a quiet, unassuming personality." (42) The arming of the Amazons depended on the circumstances at the end of the 19th century. During one of the attempts made by French ships to conquer the country which ended, in 1892 with the taking of the capital, Abomey, it was reported, in 1890, that beside a Dahomey cannon, whose operators had been killed, the body was found of the "personal Amazon" of the king, Nausica, who only the previous year had danced at court before the French Ambassador, Bayol.

The German newspaper *Post* in its report on this incident on 25th August 1892, said of the women's regiments in Dahomey: "The so-called Amazons form the bodyguard of the king, live in his palace … and are recruited from among the daughters of the leaders and among the young prison population. They are called 'Minos', which is the equivalent of 'our mother', or 'women of the king', but they live celibate lives, which has not, in the past, prevented a female commander from producing a son for the king. They wear a short-sleeved blouse, in peacetime short trousers with an apron, in times of war, long trousers; their headwear consists of a bonnet with an animal embroidered on it."

Undoubtedly these Amazons are of great ethnological interest. In all regions where traces of a matrilinear-based system persisted, evidence could be found of the existence of Amazons, and this included South America, where their discovery created such a stir that they were called after the great Amazon river. In Africa genuine Amazons only existed in very rare cases. The armed bodyguards of the rulers, women's regiments, female officers and commanders—all these fascinating phenomena—are merely remains of an old matrilinear system. Nevertheless these are evidence of the fact that large numbers of women in former times and in individual regions (in Dahomey until the end of the 19th century) were regarded as more capable on the battlefield than men, and the spread of a patrilinear-based system by no means meant that women automatically were given a subordinate position in society, not even where such prestigious positions as those of guards or warriors were concerned.

Life in the towns of the old kingdoms

Economic development and the increased political importance of certain centres in Africa south of the Sahara led at an early stage to the emergence of large towns with 100,000 and more inhabitants. Thus, in the region of the Yoruba (West Africa), many towns developed between the 12th and 14th centuries, and archaeological finds provide details of their appearance. These discoveries, combined with reports found in old travellers' descriptions, allow us to reconstruct an accurate picture of these towns, which developed at the crossroads of important trading routes.

Islamic historians of the 14th and 15th centuries give glowing accounts of the splendour of the royal cities in the Islamized parts of western Sudan. One of the oldest such descriptions to circulate in Europe comes from *Johann Leo the African's Description of Africa*, from the year 1526. Traders from the flourishing centres of the Netherlands, who were accustomed to the hustle and bustle of European trading cities visited the coast of Guinea in the 17th and 18th centuries and were impressed by the African cities. Many pictures and sketches based on their descriptions were produced, and they represent an important source of information for historians. The houses of the kings and tribal chiefs and leaders, buildings associated with religious cults, and assembly halls—all catch the eye on account of their sheer size and splendour. Olfert Dapper, in a book published in 1669, which gives a description of the African countries, passes on an eyewitness account by the merchant Samuel Bloemert, who reported of the royal palace in Benin: "It is as large as the town of Harlem, and surrounded by a special wall. The palace consists of countless splendid buildings and superb rectangular galleries of almost the same proportions as the stock-exchange in Amsterdam ... The roof of these galleries sits on wooden pillars which are clad from top to bottom in copper engraved with depictions of heroic deeds and battles ... Most of these royal buildings are covered with palm leaves which look like rectangular plates. Every roof is decorated with a pointed turret on which an extremely realistic copper statue of a bird with outstretched wings stands." (10) The book contains copperplate engravings, one of which depicts Benin, with the royal palace in the background. One can see three rectangular buildings with pitched, gabled roofs, the ridges of which have, roughly in the middle, py-

HAEUSER ZU BENIN, NEBST IHREN HINRICHTUNGEN UND IHRER ART ZU REUTEN.

48

In towns, women's sphere of activity was often limited to household duties and thus—especially in areas under Islamic influence—inequality between the sexes was created. Benin. In foreground: everyday scenes; in background: an execution scene. From: *General History of Voyages by Land and Sea ...*, Leipzig 1747. Forschungsbibliothek Gotha.

ramidal turrets on square bases, on which the figures of birds sit. Connected to these buildings are long, low wings with pitched roofs which clearly surround a central administrative building. The accuracy of this picture is corroborated not only by the description given in the surrounding text but also by later archaeological finds of bronze objects. In particular a bronze plate and a bronze casket were found which bore depictions of the palace gates and the palace itself. But the most extraordinary aspect of the royal palace in Benin must have been the way the walls, roofs, pillars and columns were all clad in bronze plate, which gleamed in the sun. Two types of bronze products were used for this: smooth plates for the roofs, and bas relief panels with ornaments or figured decorations for the walls. Some panels showed individual figures, others whole groups relating to one central plot.

The traveller Robert Norries described the royal city of the king of Dahomey as the home of 24,000 inhabitants. "The houses of each family consist of a number of small huts for the women, and one or two large rooms for the man of the house, all of which are surrounded by a high mud wall. The entire city is surrounded by a broad and deep ditch; but there are no ramparts. At four points wooden bridges span this ditch, each guarded by a watch-house in which soldiers are posted." (25)

All reports describe royal palaces and sacred buildings such as mosques, the small huts of shopkeepers and craftsmen, market places at which food and other goods were put up for sale and "celebrations", such as dances, took place. One free space was used for public council meetings and for the judgement of disputes. According to Ludewig Ferdinand Römer, all settlements which were designated as towns had, in their centre, a building open to all sides which served as town-hall. Here the palavers, or public discussions or negotiations took place. Just as individual houses or groups of houses were surrounded by walls, so, too, the entire town was protected by a mud wall or a strong pallisade. Leo the African informs us that in

Timbuktu the spacious town was enhanced by the presence of countless fresh-water fountains. By the start of the 20th century, many once famous towns south of the Sahara were in ruins or had become little more than large villages. Thus Benin was finally reduced to ashes by the English towards the end of the 19th century.

The fact cannot be ignored that with the development of towns and the spread of Islam and Christianity the position of women changed for the worse, even though their actual social degradation occured rather later, with the start of the colonial period, which had considerable impact on marriage and family life, largely through the overseas slave trade after the 16th century and the increase in itinerant workers after the middle of the 19th century. The following pages document the general framework for the socio-economic and legal position of women in an urban culture.

The towns and cities in the kingdoms grew up on the basis of the second, in some cases third, great social division of labour which went hand in hand with the world-wide development of metal extraction and processing and the (early) cultivation of the fields. Field cultivation, in contrast to basic crop cultivation, involved the use of animals for tilling, and their breeding and care played an important ancillary role. While the use of the plough only occurred in parts of the Sudan and in Ethiopia prior to the beginning of the period of colonization by Europeans in the 16th century, metal extraction and processing started much earlier. For the Sudan area it is now assumed that the working of iron began separately during the first thousand years B.C. and spread throughout West, East and the northern areas of Africa. Individual forms of extraction were developed. In the valley of the Nok culture, the area to the north of the Benue and the Niger, which is Nigeria today, metal products have been found at great depths which have been dated as coming from the first thousand years B.C.—fragments of the nozzles of bellows, iron slag, and remains of smelt-

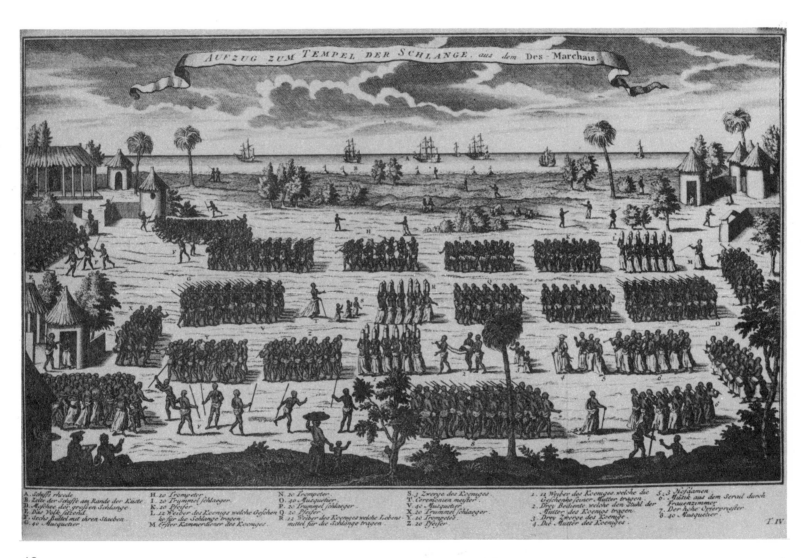

49

Women's role in traditional rites and ceremonies matched their position in religious traditions. In many areas African women were able, despite the advance of patrilinear systems, to maintain their freedoms. Traditional procession. West Africa. From: *General History of Voyages by Land and Sea* ..., Leipzig 1747. Forschungsbibliothek Gotha.

The Legal Situation

ing ovens which point to the production of iron and tin; also terracotta statuettes, which display an astonishing artistic sophistication. The introduction of iron in West Africa brought about considerable upheavals which resulted in the emergence of the Nok culture, (named after the place of discovery of various artefacts), which constituted one of the most significant cultural developments after 500 B.C.

Both important occurrences—the beginning of the working of metal and the start of the rearing of working animals—were, given the natural division of labour between the sexes which already existed, the domain of the man. The rapid development of the forces of production and the accumulation of goods which became possible, led to the second and third great social division of labour, which changed the role distribution between the sexes to the advantage of the men and strengthened the patrilinear elements in traditional African society. The second division of labour took place with the separation of the work of craftsmen from agricultural activities. This led to the production of goods for the market-place. The third division of labour consisted of the development of the separate role of trader as mediator between producer and consumer. While the natural division of labour between the sexes towards the end of the phase of primitive society gave women a respected position in the production process, their role in the processes leading to the establishment of towns and of an urban culture remained subordinate to that of men.

Towns, with their remarkable division into specialized elements—officials, scholars, craftsmen, traders, and servants, fulfilled a role as royal residences, centres for local, far-flung and transit trade, and for craftwork and culture among a majority of people who were still concerned with tilling the land and raising animals. Towns became centres of wealth and of social inequality. The gap between country and urban populations increased, accompanied by a very specific development: towns encouraged the development of patrilinearity and of new norms which gave women a subordinate position within a marriage and the family, together with new customs which favoured the dominance of men. These developments were strongly supported by the new monotheistic religions of Islam and Christianity. At this time of social change it was of considerable significance for the legal position of women in general that the urban population remained a very small minority for many centuries.

With the spread of the Islamic religion and culture came a golden age for urban cultures in West and East Africa. In Timbuktu, Djenne and other towns there developed a system of money, a banking system, and money-lending; craftsmanship and trade flourished, as did the education system, which contributed to the golden age of Islamic culture in the 8th to the 13th centuries, in which Islamic art and science, in particular mathematics, geography, astronomy, medicine and chemistry and political sciences were unique throughout the world. In the large towns mosques were built, and schools and other religious institutions founded. In the capitals of the states of Mali, Songhai, and Kanem-Bornu enormous mosques were constructed and many Koranic schools set up. The towns of Gao and Timbuktu became famous centres of Koranic learning. In the 12th and 13th centuries the university in Timbuktu, with more than 100 scholars and extensive libraries, together with that of El Azhar in Egypt was one of the strongholds of Islamic culture. Although Islam spread mainly in the towns, as time passed, mosques also were built in the villages and settlements.

Islam and Christianity forced out the old traditions. In the towns, new norms developed under Islamic influence, which covered not only such matters as the daily prayer duties, fasting during Ramadan and the avoidance of alcohol and pork, but also other day-to-day matters. Thus, among the Islamized urban upper classes, the opinion of the woman was not called for in family matters. The birth of a girl was not a matter for celebration, while the birth of a son was greeted with many good wishes for a prosperous future. Usually, in-

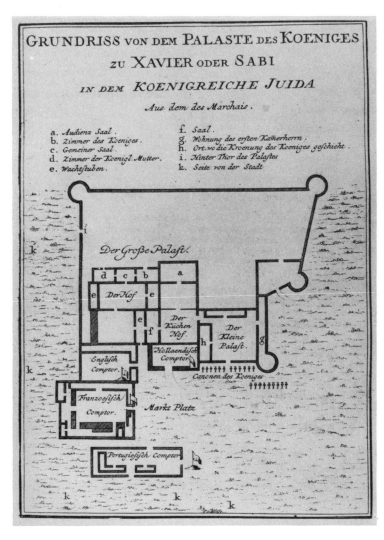

GRUNDRISS VON DEM PALASTE DES KOENIGES
zu XAVIER ODER SABI

IN DEM KOENIGREICHE JUIDA

Aus dem des Marchais.

a. Audienz Saal.
b. Zimmer des Koeniges.
c. Gemeiner Saal.
d. Zimmer der Koenigl. Mutter.
e. Wachtstuben.

f. Saal.
g. Wohnung des ersten Kämerherrn.
h. Ort, wo die Kroenung des Koeniges geschieht.
i. Hinter Thor des Palastes.
k. Seite von der Stadt.

Der Große Palast.

Der Hof.

Der Küchen Hof.

Der Kleine Palast.

Englisch Comptor.

Hollaendisch Comptor.

Canonen des Koeniges.

Franzoesisch Comptor.

Markt Platz.

Portugiesisch Comptor.

50

A glimpse into the living conditions of privileged African women is given by the ground plan of the palaces. Ground plan of the Royal Palace at Xavier or Sabi in the kingdom of Juida. From: *General History of Voyages by Land and Sea* ..., Leipzig 1747. Forschungsbibliothek Gotha.

heritance went to the sons. A woman accused of infidelity was publicly beaten or even banished to the desert. The Coptic Christian tradition in Ethiopia exercised a similar influence.

Islam and Christianity gave rise to a new awareness of time, which was expressed in the liturgical and historical calculation of time, while the everyday life of the rural community was still regulated by the rhythms of nature. Ideas arose of a present or future kingdom of heaven and the course of the world from the Creation to the Last Judgement, both notions characteristic for Christianity. The Ethiopians observed the Old Testament rules on eating whereby it was forbidden not only to partake of pork or fowl, but also to eat the flesh of hippopotamuses, elephants, camels, donkeys, mules or horses. Religious services and fasts were important elements in the struggle for personal salvation. The motto was: "Fasting and prayer are arrows against Satan."

In the towns, women often were reduced to a position of isolation, separation, and became little more than cheap labour within the home or a source of auxiliary labour to men in the home workshop, shop or small trading firm. For the socially privileged female town dweller, it was regarded as immoral to work outside the home. The rights of women were curtailed, and inequalities in productive activities were strengthened by discrimination in other spheres. A woman in an Islamized society often had to receive her husband's permission before she could leave the home, enter public places or speak with whom she wished. Often her face had to be carefully hidden from other people's gaze. E. Hopen made a careful study of the Fulbe in northern Nigeria: "The unquestionable authority of the man in his own home was supported by the entire system of laws determining a Mohammedan society."

He described a typical family scene: "When the woman handed her husband the meal, she knelt in front of him. She carefully took the water vessel, put the food at his feet and withdrew immediately, in order not to witness him eating. The woman was not permitted to call her husband directly by his name, and was not allowed to speak until he spoke to her."

For the woman in the urban lower classes there was usually no such complete break with rural conditions, and physical work remained the determining factor for her. As the family became involved in market exchanges, the woman's work retained its social importance. It must also not be forgotten that, in addition to the social degradation which actually occurred more for the women in wealthy circles than for the less well-off, there were new possibilities for women which emerged in work and social life, for example in the markets.

Another important factor was the fact that the towns, like the villages, were surrounded by well-laid out gardens and fields, and the female African urban dwellers continued to be involved in the growing of root crops, the making of clothes from plant fibres, and the creating of the raw materials for pottery and other domestic artefacts.

There was a smooth transition from rural to town architecture. As the method of construction of African houses did not allow for room divisions, and there were many women, each of them had her own hut, which nevertheless all belonged to one family and were surrounded by a pallisade of woven bamboo. A number of such compounds, with corridors between them made up a large village or a town. From a distance such settlements usually looked like a number of "large ant-hills". Usually the only external difference between a town and a village was size and the existence of a number of larger, more prominent buildings which served political, economic and cultural purposes. Often European travellers mistakenly drew the conclusion that African towns were nothing more than "large villages". Even at the beginning of the 20th century the towns of Ethiopia were hardly distinguishable, as regards the method of building, from rural villages. In both, there were round huts with walls built of clay or stone, a conical straw roof and

outhouses of a similar shape, all protected by a clay wall or a woven pallisade. The courtyards were round, and when they adjoined other ones this gave rise to half-moon shapes.

The architecture of the African peoples was very varied and consisted of more than merely the external appearance of a town, which was like a collection of huts. It reflected historical, geographical and ethnic factors, differing systems of government, religions and socio-economic situations. Towns built largely of clay, such as Timbuktu, produced, as an ensemble, completely new qualities. In addition to the mosque, in the Islamic influenced regions, one could also find, early on, in the very centre of the territory of Ethiopia, rectangular Christian churches in the Byzantine style.

It is worth while looking at the style of living in these houses, as this brings out clearly the differentiation according to social possessions within the towns, and also the particular layout and organization of the interiors. A plan of a home can thus furnish us with information about the family structure in the towns of the old empires.

Remains of these once large towns were discovered by the Europeans in the 19th century, and it was possible to distinguish houses with water-pools and inner courtyards. On the basis of the floor coverings it was possible to establish the method of construction of the oldest urban houses. One characteristic of Yoruba (West Africa) houses was the verandah on massive wooden pillars and *impluvia*—water-collecting cisterns—in the open inner courtyard. Yoruba houses for several families were of considerable dimensions. A layout reproduced by L. Frobenius shows that a typical house of this sort consisted of a rectangular building of compressed clay with a surface area of 23 × 40 metres. There was one single door to the street. Most of the space was taken up by an entrance courtyard from which doors led to 19 rooms, which covered the entire area of the courtyard. On all four sides of the courtyard there were the pillared verandahs. The rooms stretching the length of the courtyard on the left-hand

Strafe einer von den Weibern des Koeniges und ihres Liebhabers
zu Juida.

51

If traditional morality was transgressed against, the punishments were
harsh. Punishment for adultery in a public market-place. West Africa.
From: *General History of Voyages by Land and Sea* ..., Leipzig 1747.
Forschungsbibliothek Gotha.

The Legal Situation

side were for married children and their families. The head of the family and his wives lived in the main rooms, which lead to small back courtyards with *impluvia* in the middle and verandahs along the edges. The cisterns were connected by a channel and drained outside the building. In the centre of the large entrance courtyard was the house shrine, surrounded by a verandah.

In Ethiopia the better-off had spacious houses and rooms. On the floors were Persian carpets and cushions, and there were chairs for sitting on. However, most houses were small, without timbering, and lacking in elegance; usually they were round and covered with earth and straw. Houses in the Congo and in Angola were similar. Here, too, the houses of the more wealthy were roomier, their furnishings more lavish and the various rooms were decorated with mats in various colours. Of Madagascar it is known that the wealthy lived in large houses consisting of two halls and four rooms. Smaller huts for the wives and the family surrounded the main building. Carpets covered the floor and also served as wall decorations. In the houses there were iron cooking pots, wooden bowls and spoons, buckets for fetching water, small and large knives, small tweezers for removing thorns from feet and for pulling out hairs, large butcher's knives for killing the animals, iron forks for taking food out of the pots, mortars for grinding rice, wooden sieves, and large stone jars for preparing mead.

The exact nature of the building depended on the structure of the family, as the Englishman John Matthew reported, in 1785, of Sierra Leone. Everyone chose a place and "built thereon a number of small houses according to the number of his wives and others (for each wife must have her own house), all these together form a circle which is surrounded by a pallisade ... Lowly people, slaves and children sleep on mats or dried animal skins which are spread out on the ground by the fire. The more important, however, have their own sleeping places, formed by four posts set into the ground. Underneath there is a layer of

split reeds or bamboo, and mats are hung round instead of curtains. The men's dwellings contain a box in which they keep their clothes and valuables, a mat or skin on which to sit, and their weapons. In the women's quarters, however, one can find all their household utensils, mats, seats and, especially, always, a mirror." (21) Other traveller's accounts give similar descriptions of the influence of family structure on the arrangement of the dwellings. Such accounts only allow us to gain a very general impression of the living conditions of women as a mirror of their social position. However, all sources stress the new quality of urban living.

Clapperton gave a comprehensive description of town life in the kingdom of Bornu (West Africa) in the year 1822: "The walls consist of red clay and are quite smooth, the ceiling is tastefully vaulted with tree branches and covered with grass on the outside. Horns of gazelles and antelopes are used instead of nails and hooks; at various points they stick out from the walls and quivers, bows, spears and shields hang on them. A man of distinction often has four such terraces and eight turrets which form the side of his house, and the rooms for the women are underneath. Not just the people *en activité* (as the French would say) but also those who are no longer leading active lives are given homes. Horses and other animals usually have their own quarters next to one of the entrances to the courtyard. However, such houses are not usual; most of the Bornu have one of four basic types: huts made entirely of straw, with round walls made of clay with a straw roof, or made from coarse mats woven out of grasses ..." (37)

According to P. Antonio Zucchelli the wealthy inhabitants of the Congo had handsome and comfortable residences. These included sleeping places, while the poor merely slept on a mat. But even the wealthy spent most of their lives in the open air, as they usually remained outside in the courtyard, sitting, eating and sleeping, even when they were ill, except at those times when it rained, "when they withdraw to a type of hall built like a summerhouse, roofed over but open at the sides, so that the air can circulate." The dwellings of the urban lower classes were not very different from those of the rural dwellers. The same author reported that in the Congo the entire domestic equipment consisted of "some bowls for cooking in, some containers for carrying water", a hoe, a chopper and similar utensils. Because of the lack of stones, they usually had to construct their houses with palm branches which they anchored firmly in the ground, or with reeds and other materials, which they skillfully wove into walls. It was only possible to stand upright in the centre of the room, and if one stretched one's arms out one could touch the walls. (15)

Abbé Demanet gave a description of the dwellings and household utensils of the simple people of West Africa: "The huts of the negroes are round and pointed at the top. They have no windows whatsoever and what light they have comes in through the door, which is extremely low. They rest on stakes driven into the ground and linked with crossbeams. To these they fix poles which serve as rafters and meet at the top to form the point. These are covered with straw, reeds or a sort of withy which grows commonly throughout the country. The huts very soon become black on the inside, on account of the fire which burns continuously for the cooking of rice or millet." Household implements only took up little space, consisting merely of some earthenware pots, calabashes (containers made of pumpkins), baskets and one or two other objects.

Details of house construction and the forms taken by dwellings are an important historical source, for they reflect the social pattern of urban life and the patrilinear elements in its development, which had a decisive influence on the legal and actual position of African women.

LOVE, MARRIAGE AND FAMILY

Family and society

Abbé Demanet, who worked for some time as a missionary in West Africa, published a travel report in 1778 in which he expressed great enthusiasm for the native traditions and customs:

"It is unusual to come across the type of conflicts and contradictions which the European nations inflict upon themselves among these people. They are not subject to either excesses of envy and jealousy, or to attacks of greed. The goods and titles which are so sought after in our countries hold no attraction for them; rank, pomp, ceremony, and compliments seem to them idiotic or a form of martyrdom." (20)

The structure of their daily life was the outcome of a long path of development, in which both women and men had played an equal role. The typical characteristics of their way of life and ways of communication were reflected not only in their way of eating, greeting each other, celebrating holidays, burying their dead, but particularly in marriage and the family.

Paul Herman Isert paints an enthusiastic picture of religion, way of life, and care for the sick. He does, however, make a clear distinction between the Africans who were still untouched by the European slave trade, and those who lived on the coast and were in close contact with Europeans. Isert spent six years (1783–1789) on the Gold Coast (Ghana). In a manner similar to that of Rousseau he painted a glowing picture of life in the interior, of people who "lived in almost the same simplicity of style as our earliest forefa-

thers", of regions where "there were signs of innocence everywhere and the most honest people", where "crimes such as murder and theft were unknown". He then compared these intact relations and forms of behaviour with those he encountered around the European trading settlements on the coast, and came to the bitter conclusion that, "it is therefore the enlightened nations, the Europeans, the Christians, who have taught the Africans this type of behaviour and accustomed them to all sorts of crimes." (23)

In the book *Carl Bernhard Wadström's Treatise on the Colonies, in particular on the West Coast of Africa,* the originally high level of the African daily and family life and the evaluation of it by European participants in the slave trade was given the following appraisal: "In order that this important moral appraisal be carried out with total objectivity the observer must not be swayed by any preconceptions; he must keep an open mind in order to soak in the full and beautiful impression of everything around him. Every reasonable person will appreciate the necessity of this once he realizes what a false picture has been painted of these people by those who transform them into commercial objects and then try to justify their own attrocious behaviour by slandering them." (29) In the evaluation of "African" relations in earlier centuries one should keep in mind the forms of co-existence of the sexes prevalent in Europe at the same time.

What were the inter-relations between family and society? How did matrilinearity first express itself? What were the consequences of the transition to patrilinearity?

The position of women provides new, sometimes surprising insights into traditional thought and customs. However, external factors, especially the effects of colonial-feudal and forms of colonial-capitalist rule and exploitation left their mark on the life of the traditional African family.

The whole of life, birth, upbringing, love, weddings, marriage and the family, right up to death, revolved round the tribe. Women and men felt a duty towards the larger family and the village community. A number of large families, which were in some way related to each other, belonged to a tribe, which had its own settlement, a local culture, often a local language, local religious beliefs, rites, dances and games, common local feast-days. Their ideals and values corresponded to a way of behaviour which in earlier times, on a lower socio-economic level and under the influence of matrilinearity, had a significant and on the whole positive function—women knew about mutual dependency and they expressed this knowledge in common work, in the administration of justice, in wisdom, self control and the use of dialogue; they watched over the rules, norms, customs and traditions which were taking root in the family group.

Reitzenstein pointed out that the word "family" had not long been introduced into the language. "Family comes from the same root as famulus, servant, slave …" (126) It was in the family, as the basic social and economic unit within which the personality of the individual develops, that the various development forms of close economic and work-cooperation between the sexes (all the same whether they were structured in a matrilinear or patrilinear way) were given expression.

In the course of historical development, the single social cells which were originally based on blood relations, have gradually lost their significance. This occurred with the formation of the state organization and was especially true of those organizational forms which were based on individual families and extended families: tribes and clans.

52

This cliff drawing shows a meeting. Rock engravings appeared as early as 8 thousand years B.C., while others were still being produced in the 18th and 19th centuries.

In Africa, the family first appeared as the extended family, and encompassed three or four generations, forming a living and economic community. Although it went through various stages of development, nowhere did it take on the form of the monogamous single family—this was a later historical product.

It is worth stressing that within the extended family the women were often a common possession. A woman from outside who was wooed successfully by a younger member of the family, belonged also to the male head of the family, who held authority over the whole unit. The so-called "hospitality prostitution" was derived from this: the right to the commonly-owned woman was extended to guests.

With the transition to the polygamous, patriarchal, extended family women and servants had the same standing, although this should not be seen particularly as a down-grading of women.

There are numerous examples of how the majority of African women, even when there was obvious male dominance (also in many nomadic tribes), despite their formal lack of rights, managed in practice to assert themselves. In the collection of *Fairy tales of the Chi people on the Gold Coast* (Ghana) which are attributed to the African Christian I. Adaye, translated by the missionary I. Bellon and published in 1914 in the *Material for the Seminar on Oriental Languages in Berlin*, edited by Prof. Dr. C. Velten and Prof. D. Westermann, there is a fairy tale in which there is already a rebellious note to be detected in the treatment of love and marriage. "Nobody knows what a woman thinks", is how the publishers entitled the story, which tells of the love between a pretty girl and a young boy. The father of the girl, however, gives away his daughter to a king living in a polygamy to be his wife. But the two lovers manage, with stealth, to carry on their relationship without the legitimate husband knowing.

It may not be possible to present the whole complicated structure in which the development of the family took place, but it is possible to set out the basic differences between the ethnic groups within the old kingdoms and the primitive social forms, and to discuss the concepts of tribe and clan.

The tribe was a group of people which existed mainly in the primitive or pre-class society, and which has its own name, often its own language or dialect, a common territory and a common culture.

The tribes were divided into clans. A "clan" was a group of relatives, in which the men (patriclan) or the women (matriclan) could trace their ancestry through one or several common ancestors, and within a territorial unit also formed a political unit. The term "gens" is often interpreted in the same or in a similar way. Several extended families formed a clan, which was often identical to a village community.

The unfettered individualism of the bourgeois society was alien to the inhabitants of old Africa. The law of solidarity—albeit on an ethnic basis—played a significant role. This was not just a case of the proverbial African hospitality.

In contrast to the primitive social tribes with their groups of relatives, the people in the old kingdoms were bound together mainly by economic and cultural links of a neighbouring territorial nature. They were also separated by differing shares of property and wealth. Belonging to a kingdom did not necessarily mean that the African peoples lacked a "local consciousness". There was a clear gentile element which provided the foundation for the tribes and the tribal consciousness.

Paul Herman Isert wrote about social coherence in the family, the village community, the tribe and religious organization, about the ideal of equality of property and sharing with others:

"It cannot be said that there are poor people among them. Every house or family has to look after its own members and if one of its members suffers from need, then the whole family must do likewise. There can probably be no poverty here other than that arising from a long drought, but there are always plenty of fish to be found in the sea and an abundance of game in the forests." (23)

The "religious world-view" in old Africa and the religious basis to the social order had a decisive influence on the ethical, moral and social values of the culture, which in the inter-relationship between individual and community gave preference to the latter. This of course included the recognition that life remains primarily individual. However, life was also understood to be communal, and the comparison with nature came to the fore: As in nature, society represented a whole, but every individual acquired his meaning and significance only from the general, every member of the family, of the clan and the tribe knew from the start that he/she did not just live his/her own life, but that of the whole community. If separated from the whole, the individual could not exist.

It can only be briefly mentioned here that ethnic solidarity, with its restriction to family, group and tribe, held the personality in a tight straightjacket, and isolated it from the rest of the world. The ethical value system encouraged the rise of privileged groups within the tribal structures. The principle of respect for the elderly and the first child (the hierarchical way of thought) was later exploited by the chiefs and other social elites to serve their own purposes, and tribal thinking, together with ethnic solidarity, led to indifference to the fate of the neighbouring tribes or even to open hostility. Such developments and tendencies were evident by the end of the 18th century.

The stubborn fettering of the woman to the traditional extended family, clan and tribe had a negative effect on the living conditions of the African woman. The more positive aspects of the original gentile conditions have assumed a more negative content in recent times. The overwhelming majority of women are employed in agriculture and as a rule earn nothing, because women only work the fields to cover the needs of the family. Throughout the colonial period, due to the view of role-division between man and woman fostered by this period, women are often placed in a position of subordination and dependence for the whole of their lives. Whether divorced or widowed, they lose

Die Madegaßen oder Madagaskaren.

53

Young couple. Book illustration. Madagascar. From: *General History of Voyages by Land and Sea ...*, Leipzig 1747. Forschungsbibliothek Gotha.

property and children to their previous husband or to his family. Contraception for minors and family planning are taboo.

Premarital relationships and marriage

Polygamy was practised not only in the Islamic parts of Africa but also in other parts of the Continent. Prosperous men had several wives (polygyny), and it was not unusual for a chief's status to be partly determined by the number of wives he had. The man usually had to build every wife her own hut, which belonged to her alone and where the husband visited her. Polyandry, when a woman had several husbands, also existed for some time, particularly in the interior of Africa, but it was so rare that it hardly had any impact on the impressions of European travellers.

At the end of the 19th century, four-fifths of humanity was still living in polygamies, whereas, for the other fifth, monogamy was a legal requirement, which did not, however, exclude certain liaisons with other women.

It is not the form of marriage that existed in African states which is decisive for judging social and moral relations, but the fact that the living together of the sexes had already been given a social cloak, before the first travellers from the ancient world, or Islamic and European travellers had come in contact with the daily life of the Africans.

A prerequisite for marriage was the existence of a meaningful Common Law and a developed religious consciousness. Marriage provides evidence of developed socio-economic relations, of the existence of land cultivation and cattle farming and of specialized activities such as crafts and trading. One purpose of marriage was to assert rights over children and thus to assert ownership of property and to enlarge property. Thus marriage originally served primarily social demands and was a social institution, which in the time

of the old African kingdoms was firmly rooted in the people's consciousness. Content and form of the marriage were determined by the existing socio-economic and historical circumstances. In practice, polygamy became less common as soon as the socio-economic relations which had brought it about changed.

There were quite a few European travellers who gave glowing reports of marriage in old Africa even in the 18th and 19th centuries.

Unreserved approval is expressed in the *History of Loango, Kakongo and other kingdoms of Africa* written by Abbé Proyart at the end of the 18th century. According to him, the unpublished reports of French missionaries show that "the greatest purity and lack of affectation in manners, a holy and steadfast attitude to marriage, rare occurrence of adultery and divorce, modesty and restraint in young unmarried persons, good behaviour and decency in all their pleasures" could be attributed to the Africans. "The portraits painted by almost every other traveller among the negro peoples from Senegal right down to Angola are quite different. They almost all complain about the appalling immoral behaviour of unmarried people of both sexes, claiming that in many countries indecent behaviour has come to be looked upon as a merit and single women count the number of men they sleep with as a sign of their beauty, or offer it as a recommendation to prospective husbands. Adultery is supposed to be so frequent and normal, that unfaithfulness has become the norm, and men and fathers take it as an insult if strangers reject the wives and daughters offered to them ... Most writers who have visited the west coast of Africa and have described it, only knew peoples who were either contaminated by contact with Europeans, were embittered by great cruelty, or had lost all humanity through the slave trade, and were so hardened to all the criminality arising out of it that they had to find in them such monsters as they described in their writings." (19)

At another point in his book the Abbé expresses his opinion in an even more forthright manner: "It is the generally held opinion, and one which is being given more and more credibility, that the loss of morals among these peoples has become totally boundless; at least this is how the new writers describe these countries. People who claim to be travellers have abused the gullibility of the public and are not ashamed to claim that whoring, adultery, and the most outrageous excesses are part of the customs of the country, that the men actually encourage unfaithfulness among women and that even burial ceremonies involve the most scandalous acts. An author who writes for his living pays little attention to the truth if it is to his advantage to conceal it, and that is often the case. He is certain to please the numerous flippant readers with such sumptuous tales. The readers soak up everything which enobles their iniquities, or seems to spread the power of the passions that rule them over a greater number of people. And yet these are such slanderous reports, on which systems are built up, and according to which we are most ceremoniously assured, that the Christian religion cannot be the religion of all the world, and that the chastity which it preaches means that it will never take root in the lands of the midday sun and the hot equatorial belt …" (19)

The argumentative churchman did not content himself with polemics, but also painted a picture of good manners and the high moral qualities of women. Abbé Proyart offered in his work a brave example of an attempt to counteract the mistaken idea that the exotic strangeness which the Europeans met in Africa, was reason enough for negative criteria to be used in the evaluation of African cultures.

Marriage, i.e. a lasting attachment sealed by certain rites, can be traced back into the first years of the old states. It did, however, exist alongside other types of relations, and marriage ties were more frequent among the elite and privileged or the elderly than among simple people and young people.

A large number of sources from the 18th and 19th centuries provide evidence of unlimited sexual relations between the younger members of the tribes

Kleidung der Schwarzen auf dem grünen Vorgebürge.

54

Family scene. West Africa. From: *General History of Voyages by Land and Sea …*, Leipzig 1747. Forschungsbibliothek Gotha.

in old Africa, but marriage seemed to put an end to other relationships. On the other hand, there were reports of great importance being attached to a new wife's virginity being intact; if a man found that she was not a virgin, he could send her back to her parents. Divorce was also possible.

The content and form of marriage went through great changes, and depending on the historical, regional and social conditions, on the strength of the tribe's influence and other factors, there were various ways in which a man and woman could live together.

It was a rule that marriage did not take place within the same gens, but outside the tribe. There are examples of primitive and of developed forms of marriage. It was based on old matriarchal relations if the woman stayed in her tribe and the man only visited her from time to time; the children then belonged to their mother's tribe. Or the man entered the woman's tribe or at least stayed there for some time, in order to work for his wife's relatives (so-called service marriage). This type of marriage took place without any "bride money" being exchanged. Brodie Cruickshank gives the following report: "Among the poorer classes man and woman live for a while together, without a dowry being paid. At most a bottle of rum is bought for friends to drink at the wedding feast. In such cases the man usually lives with the bride's family and offers his services to them in order to cover both of their living costs." (43)

The marriage rules did not change with the rise of patriarchy. The marriage partner continued to be chosen from outside of the gens, outside of the tribe, but the woman was incorporated into the man's tribe. The man paid a contribution in the form of hunting booty, weapons and so on, as a type of compensation payment, or he did specific services for the girl's father once the girl had already been removed from her clan.

This "payment for the bride" was one of the most widespread customs. The bought marriage was the most common form of getting married. This was without a doubt also the basis for European marriages until recent times, as is pointed out by Abbé Demanet: "Those fathers who have daughters are in this respect much better off than their European counterparts, who have to give money or some equivalent in order to get rid of them. In Africa they receive money from those looking for wives." (20)

The woman could also be the active partner in starting up a relationship. The previously mentioned H. C. Monrad, who lived in West Africa from 1805 to 1809 informs us that, "although the negresses do not exactly egg on the negroes, they make their wishes quite clear. If they are in love with a man, they send him a dish of tasty food with pytto or palm wine. He understands this sort of hint and follows it up if he feels so inclined." (36)

Premarital relations were a matter of mutual consent. The Englishman Brodie Cruickshank reported in 1855 after his 18-year stay on the Gold Coast, that women and men were capable of tender passion, which was "characterized by order and decency, was full of painstaking care and doubt and sought satisfaction without paying any attention to the huge sacrifices which it may bring." Cruickshank continued poetically: "The African calls out the name of his loved one, in order to muster up courage when he is about to throw himself into the thick of a battle; the canoe-rower lifts his oar with new energy on calling out her name; the tired hammock-carrier soaks up new energy through the same all-powerful magic word, and the lonely traveller fights the monotony of his way by singing a song in her praise. As we sat round our camp-fire in Apollonia, we often listened with anticipation and pleasure to the tender descriptions of home and the loved one, in which they liked to let their fantasy take over and in which they expressed the thought and the hope that they, on their homecoming, would be met with increased tenderness and affection from their lovers and wives because of the dangers they had survived."

House of a family in
Senegambia in *Johann
Leo the African's Description of Africa.* Forschungsbibliothek Gotha.

Wohnung eines Negers in Senegambien.

56

The many mother-and-child representations symbolize social values. Figure of woman with child. Sculpture. Mayombe, Zaïre. Museum für Völkerkunde, Hamburg.

57 a and b

Seat of a chief with representations of love. Wood. East Africa. Museum für Völkerkunde, Staatliche Museen Preussischer Kulturbesitz, Berlin (West).

58

Pregnant woman of the
Tikar. Wooden sculpture,
around 1900. Height
63 cm. Cameroon. Mu-
seum für Völkerkunde,
Dresden.

59

Stylized wooden doll which the Ashanti call "Akuaba". These were mostly small figures with an oversized, rounded, flat head, short, rudimentary hands and cylindrical rump. They were worn as amulets and were supposed to protect against infertility, assure easy childbirth and ensure the child would be healthy and well-formed. Doll. Height 34 cm. Ashanti, Ghana. Staatliches Museum für Völkerkunde, Linden-Museum, Stuttgart.

60

Carved object with magical properties for fertility. Cylinder-doll of the Ambo, Angola. Rautenstrauch-Joest-Museum, Cologne.

61

Seated woman with child.
These representations
were also supposed to
protect the child from
illness by their magical
properties. Sculpture. Ba-
samba, Zaïre. Museum
für Völkerkunde,
Hamburg.

62

The high moral qualities which women were supposed to possess meant that their depiction was particularly suited for use in religious rituals. It was assumed that a depiction of the "Original Mother" would increase the magical power of ordinary objects. The bowl being carried here served the purpose of containing the cola-nuts required for the Ifa Oracle in West Africa; these nuts were cast in front of the oracle when it was being consulted. Wooden figure of woman with child. Museum für Völkerkunde, Hamburg.

63

The beehive-shaped clay huts with ornamented surfaces are exactly as described in one of the oldest reports about the appearance of towns and villages, dating from the year 1526. Northern Cameroon.

64

Girl wearing traditional cloth. 19th century. Lepembe, Ubena Land.

65

It was not just in the village community that customs, feelings and attitudes were influenced by the rural way of life, but also in the towns. Woman with wedding ring made of tin, worn on forehead. Bamum, Cameroon.

66

Arm bangles made of wire signify that the elder brother of the girl from the Tuga tribe in Kenya has gone through the ceremony of initiation. The rows of glass beads reveal that she can already have children herself, but is not yet married.

67

Woman with child on her back. She is carrying a wooden bowl for service to Ifa. Height 21 cm. Museum für Völkerkunde, Staatliche Museen Preussischer Kulturbesitz, Berlin (West).

68

Sleeping quarters were often extremely spartan. Neck-rest. Height 19 cm. Bayaka, Congo. Rietbergmuseum, Zurich.

69

Seated woman with
child. Sculpture. Height
35.1 cm. Ashanti, Ghana.
Staatliches Museum für
Völkerkunde, Linden-
Museum, Stuttgart.

Cruickshank elaborated further: "Men and women make the greatest effort to be attractive to each other. In this respect they make themselves up with great care and indulge in the most open flirting. They often exchange tokens of their love and watch over the objects of their affection with a jealous eye. It is often the case that they fight over a loved one, and this can lead to a sharp exchange of words or they may even come to blows. Often matters of the heart are kept secret and relationships are carried on without the knowledge of relatives; however, if a man seduces a virgin, he is compelled to marry her, or if the parents do not want the marriage to take place, he has to pay for her dowry." (43) Love and mutual affection dominated the decision to get married.

The form of marriage was not a barrier to real affection, or to marriages of love rather than convenience. Even in polygamies the individual's emotions and affections played the dominant role in marriages. Everywhere the actual wedding ceremony was preceded by the wooing. Either the youth himself, his parents or one or more of his trusted friends took on this task, either because they wanted to, or simply because it was their job.

Paul Jacob Bruns wrote on this topic in 1796 with regard to the Congo: "If someone falls in love with a girl, he tries to gain the consent of the girl and her parents by making presents. If the presents are accepted by the parents the suitor need not fear a refusal from the girl. The man undertakes to marry the girl in a few years' time if she still pleases him. A widow's pension is agreed on. Once this has been settled, the man takes his loved one home and they live together." (26) And Abbé Demanet wrote: "If someone wants to take a girl to be his wife, he goes to see her parents, or if she does not have any, to see her relatives, and agrees on a price, which is appropriate to the financial circumstances of the bridegroom and to the age and beauty of the girl. On receipt of the present he is handed over the bride; but there is never any credit system. She is taken to his hut, and as soon as she en-

ters it, she is held to be his wife. After this home-bringing of the bride there follow three days of feasting and dancing, the cost of which must be covered by the young husband ..." (20)

In the south of Ethiopia, as a remnant of bygone matriarchal rule, it was still the custom that the young woman, as opposed to the future bridegroom, took the initiative in marriage. She went to the family of her chosen future husband taking a big stick with her. The bridegroom's mother took the stick and called a family meeting. If the decision was positive, the stick was planted in front of the living quarters to let everyone know.

Unrequited love was written about in legends, fairy tales, fables and proverbs. Brodie Cruickshank told of a legend which was in the form of a song about a beautiful girl on the Gold Coast: "She was the object of the all-consuming passion of a young man from Cape Coast. Her relatives thought that her charms meant that they could expect a better marriage partner, and refused to listen to his wooing. This refusal was such a blow to the young lover whose sweetest dreams had been thwarted that life became an unbearable burden to him and he decided to sacrifice himself to his passion." After parting songs and grave-side songs the girl also followed him to the grave.

Wedding and marriage were sacred in character. There was a great variety of wedding customs. The "medicine man or the magician" was present at the wedding and secret ceremonies and sacrificial rites were carried out. In *Johann Leo the African's Description of Africa* written in 1526, the wedding and marriage are mentioned: "The following customs are common for marriage: if someone wants to take a woman for his wife, and has obtained her father's permission, his father, if he is still alive, rounds up his friends and they go together with two notaries into a mosque. There, in the presence of the bride and bridegroom, they draw up a document concerning the marriage settlement and the form of the dowry." There was no mention of the purchase or sale of a bride, such as is often attributed to this period, but rather of a marriage contract. "If the bridegroom wants to take the bride home, he helps her into an octagonal, wooden stretcher, decorated with silk clothes and brocades; this is carried by special carriers on their heads as well as by the friends and relatives of both parties. It is also accompanied by much piping, trumpeting, drumming and by torch-carriers—the bridegroom's relatives go in front of the carriage, those of the bride behind. They take the road to the big market-place next to the main mosque. Here the bridegroom greets the father and the relatives of the bride, who then goes immediately to his house and waits for him in her room. Her father, brother and uncle accompany her as far as the bedroom door and present her to the bridegroom's mother. As soon as she enters the room, the bridegroom puts his foot on her's and they shut themselves in." Leo Africanus stresses the value placed on virginity; the Islamic influence can certainly be detected here as well. "Meanwhile a feast is prepared in the house; a woman stands by the door of the bedroom, and she is passed a cloth stained with blood after the marriage has been consummated. She then goes to the wedding guests and declares in a loud voice: the bride was found to be a virgin. She then gets something to eat from the bridegroom's relatives, and goes, accompanied by other women, to the house of the bride's mother, where she is also invited to eat. However, if the bride is found not to be a virgin, the bridegroom gives her back to her parents: this is held to be the greatest scandal and all those present go away without eating anything." Several feasts on different days were quite usual. "At their dances, which lasted through the whole night, there were both musicians and singers, who took it in turn to play and sing, creating a rather pleasant harmony." (3)

In Christian Ethiopia the marriage ceremony was performed with the priest's blessing at home or in front of the church door. According to Paul Jacob Bruns the marriages were "contracts which were signed for a certain period, and lasted as long as the man and woman were content with each other. Apart from the consent of both parties, no other formalities were required for the marriage to take place."

The same author writes about the relationship of a man to his wife in West Africa: "The men are pleasant to them, love them, and it is seldom the case that they mistreat them. They give them good clothing and all the finery they could wish for. They spend everything they gain from trade and travel on this. They have bracelets, rings, and earrings made from the gold they get in inner Africa and give these to their wives. They also have decorations for their sabres and knives made." (26)

The girls married young, often at the age of 11 to 13, and it was thought to be a scandal to be unmarried. The marriage age was in accordance with the earlier puberty. According to Reitzenstein the girls married:

Sudan	at the age of 12 to 14
North Guinea	at the age of 10 to 12
Mandingo	at the age of 14
Somali	at the age of 13
South East Africa	at the age of 12 to 14
Herero	at the age of 12
Nama	at the age of 8 to 9
San	at the age of 7
Madagascar	at the age of 10

Marriage did not always take place at this age, it was looked upon as a kind of engagement period in some tribes. Thus in West Africa marriage often did not take place before 18, yet it was not unusual for married couples from 15 to 17 years old already to have children.

The number of women in polygamous marriages varied considerably. Often the first wife insisted that the husband married a second wife, in order to lighten her workload. The new wives were subservient to her and served her to a certain extent. In most cases there was one main wife, often the first wife, but sometimes the one who bore the first child, mostly the first son.

The other wives were considered secondary wives. One can read about the privileged position of the first wife in Abbé Demanet: "At first all the women seem to have an equal standing in relationship to their husband, but after a while one notices, after all, differences in status. The first chosen, especially if she has sons, is the mistress of the house; she does the honours, and if she carries rank, she knows how to ensure she is treated in the manner which her position demands. She can only be dethroned if she is unfaithful: an advantage not enjoyed by the other women. They are on the contrary burdened with all the housework; if their husbands are asleep or are talking with others, they chase away the maranguins, which disturb them and put them in a temper. It is also their duty to fetch their husbands' tobacco and pipe when they awaken and hand them over with the greatest subservience."

Many authors have exaggerated polygamy or given a false impression of it. This custom was objectivized as long as it corresponded to life experiences and new social mechanisms had not yet been formed and gained sufficient authority. The life together of the two sexes in a polygamous marriage was subject to the strictest regulation.

Abbé Demanet wrote about special regulations according to which the man could only spend a certain number of days with one of his wives, a rule which has actually remained valid to this day. "If a man has several wives ..., he gives each one a hut, where she lives with her children and runs her own little household. The women on the other hand take it in turn each week to prepare his food and sleeping place. During this period they take great care not to do anything wrong, otherwise they may pay dearly for their mistakes, because their fellow wives would immediately make use of their disfavour. It is also very rare that any justified complaints are made against them. They give their husband a new garment in the fashion of the country and compete amongst each other who can spin the finest cloth and make the best dye." (20)

VERHEIRATHUNGS CEREMONIE DER HOTTENTOTTEN, aus Kolben

70

Imaginary wedding ceremony. Book illustration. Southern Africa. From: *General History of Voyages by Land and Sea ...*, Leipzig 1747. Forschungsbibliothek Gotha.

One consequence of the marriage of one man to several women, the marriage being based on a separated economy, was the division of the family into various household-communities, connected through the common husband. Although the children usually belonged by law to the father's family, they felt in practice—as in the time of matrilinearity—that they belonged to their mother and her relatives. The African woman who lived in a polygamy usually had her own property, own fields, own cattle, own house; she provided for her children from her own work and—to an exactly regulated degree—for her husband. She often used anything that was left over for trading. In south east Africa each woman had, apart from her own house, her own courtyard, garden and own tools.

There are a whole number of reasons for the survival of polygyny. The main reasons are social ones, e.g. provision for members of the family after death. The father left his wives to his son when he died, and this easily acquired wealth of wives immediately made the son's life a privileged one. The young chiefs in particular profited from this form of marriage. Another reason for living together with several wives was the fact that in some regions women were forbidden to do hard physical work during pregnancy, to hoe the field, trample grain, carry heavy loads—and this could be compensated for easily if the man had a second or third wife. It was furthermore often the case that intimate relations had to be broken off from time to time or completely during pregnancy. This was also the case after the birth, while the mother fed the baby, which could be a period of 12 to 36 months. The ruling on sexual restraint was supposed to prevent the death of the newly born child and the drying up of the mother's milk.

No less controversial than polygamy is the custom of buying a bride, which was likewise based on old social and legal traditions. In the course of time the original reason for the payment was forgotten, and with the growth of patriarchal relations it came to be understood as a sum paid for the woman herself. It was

given new names, "bride money", "bride present" etc. The payment was a custom whereby, the fiancé gave the bride's father cattle or food, later money, as a prerequisite for the coming marriage. The bride-price served a social-protection function for centuries: it made divorce more difficult, because it had to be paid back; both families continued to provide for the marriage partners in the interest of stability in the marriage; the cost of bringing the bride up were covered by this one-off payment, and it also covered the loss which a farming family suffered when a daughter left. Only with the introduction of the money-based economy and with the arbitrary raising of the price did this institution begin to crumble. It should not be forgotten that the social function of this custom went through great changes analogous to other developments in society. Together with demands for the bride price to be reduced, new forms of presents emerged, which served much the same function.

Today the bride-gift is made as a relict of a tradition, which in many places degrades the engagement to the level of pure barter. "Exchange goat or cow for wife"—this sarcastic formula is still valid in many African countries and is proof of the need to break decisively with such ancient traditions and customs, which have a very restricting effect today and serve to maintain the unequal role division between man and woman.

Polygamy and the bride-price are part of old traditions, which do still exist in the present, but no longer fit into the picture of a free and independent Africa. The same is true of arranged marriages. Wherever the relics of the ancient matriarchal rule can be traced it was felt in the consciousness of the people to be an injustice if parents (the father!) ignored the wishes of their children in matters of love and marriage.

The tendency towards arranged marriages certainly underwent a fast acceleration in Africa. With the rise of private property, the dependence of the woman on the man in marriage not only increased, but her right of decision in the choice of husband was also diminished. Fathers often gave away daughters, while they were still children, to a creditor, in order to pay off their debts. The fate of the future marriage was often decided without the consent of the young girl, and under the Islamic influence which often interfered in relations between the sexes, particularly in the more privileged sections of society, the girl frequently was not given a chance to even glimpse the face of her future husband. Life together was often reduced to the woman constantly and servilely catering to every whim of the husband.

The report of the English scientist, E. Hopen, on the people of the Fulbe in West Africa stems from a more recent period and provides evidence of relations wherein the wish to enter into marriage or to absolve a marriage was the privilege of the man. The man (father, eldest son, legal guardian) could decide the fate of the woman—to the extent of arranging her marriage. The man, as owner of numerous cattle, sheep and goats, thought only of enlarging his herds, and all family matters were made subordinate to this obsession. The divorced woman was often left without any means of survival, and the children were taken away from her. E. Hopen questioned 200 men and found that in the course of their lives they had married 480 wives. A 48-year-old man had married 21 times, a 66-year-old man 14 times. It was often the case that a man had been divorced five or more times. It has only recently been ruled by the U.N. that the consent of the partner is necessary for marriage and that the absolute power of the parents over their daughters' fate should be annulled.

The same tendency that can be observed in the form and content of marriage can also be recognized in marriage break-up. Originally both partners had equal rights. Paul Jacob Bruns wrote about Ethiopia: "If one or other of the partners no longer wishes to be tied to the contract, it is annulled and renewed as often as the interested partners desire. If a married couple decide to separate, each one of them takes back his part of the common property and the children are split between them." The same author writes at another point: "If disagreements arise between them, they separate from each other without anyone's honour being damaged." (26) The loss of women's rights in marriage break-up, which can go as far as her being kept in a sort of guardianship, is a product of a later period.

In the case of adultery, a similar tendency can be detected. The punishment for adultery was often less harsh for men than for women. According to Abbé Demanet: "If one of these women or bed-partners forgot her duty for one moment, she and her seducer were sentenced to death on the spot. In this case there was no hope of compassion." The death penalty was used for adultery in many areas, in West Africa, on the island of Madagascar or among the Nama tribes in Southern Africa. According to Paul Jacob Bruns: "The adulterer on the Gold Coast is sold (to the slave trade, H. L.) or has to buy himself out with money. If it is the wife of a well-to-do man, he has to pay the value of 3 slaves, and if she is one of the king's wives, he is executed and his family is sold."

Robert Norries reported at the end of the 18th century from Dahomey, that every "act of adultery is very severely punished, and that every unguarded act of gallantry means death or slavery for whoever took part in it." For that reason there was in that town "a certain number, appropriate to the size of the town, of women who have to make themselves available to everyone who visited them. The cost of their favours is regulated and very moderate." Norries claims that the reason for the "girls of pleasure, whose activities are given a royal seal of approval" and who had to pay a special tax, was in order to prevent the "peace of individual families being upset." (25)

Brodie Cruickshank reported in the mid-19th century from the Gold Coast: "Adultery on the part of the woman is punished by demanding money or compensation from the man and this can be anything between 1 and 10 pounds depending on the rank of the person. In a country where polygamy is so widespread, such a crime is of course quite common: some men even make money out of the weakness of their women and encourage them to be unfaithful." (43) Details on the necessity mentioned in other sources to keep women available to European traders, travellers etc. and often of whole flocks of concubines and prostitutes are described in 17th-century sources. The first report of these comes from Wilhelm Johann Müller in his report *Die Africanische, auf der Guineischen Gold-Küste gelegene Landschaft Fetu* (The African landscape of Fetu on the Guinean Gold Coast) written in 1675: "When a young man comes from Europe / indecent women soon sell themselves / who prostitute their bodies / for a small sum / be it even a bottle of brandy / they then remain with this partner / so long as he lives in this country / or travels home / then they look for another one." (12)

This is something which was associated with colonialism; it led to the African women being offered as hospitality prostitutes to strangers for small trinkets which were nevertheless highly valued. It shows quite clearly the negative effects of some external factors on the life of the Africans.

Childbirth, child-rearing and initiation

"The houses consist of several courtyards, within four walls, with rooms for the slaves: then there is a corridor and an inner courtyard, which leads to the quarters of the various wives. Every wife has a square area of her own, which is enclosed by walls and has a prettily covered hut. From there one goes up a broad staircase with five or six steps, which leads to the rooms of the man of the house: there are two buildings like towers, connected by a balcony. They look onto the street and have a barred window ..." (37) This description refers to the kingdom of Bornu and is taken from *Description of the Journey and Discoveries Made in North and Central Africa in the Years 1822 to 1824*, Weimar 1827,

by the Englishmen Denham and Clapperton. "They sleep on mats and cover themselves with animal skins. Married women are very superstitious and always make sure that their beds are covered with the skins of certain animals when their husbands come to them, and they like to believe that they can use the skins to determine what kind of child they will have. If the skin of a panther or a leopard is used as a blanket, it will either be a boy or there will be no child. If the father is a warrior and a leader, the boy will also be a soldier, brave but bloodthirsty. A lion skin actually prevents conception: although there are some exceptions ..." (37)

During pregnancy, women were forbidden to eat certain foods and, as already mentioned, had to partly or completely renounce intimate relations. This was also true for the period when they were breast-feeding a baby. It is worth mentioning the man-childbed, when the woman in childbed got up immediately after birth and the man lay down in her place to deceive the evil spirits. There were certainly other reasons for this custom being adhered to by some tribes—but this protection function was its main function. Where the man-childbed was usual, the man went through all the magic rites which were usually performed by the woman.

Among the Masai in East Africa there exist reports of a 10-day period. In places where the women spent this period in special huts, it lasted up to 22 days in West Africa and up to 40 days in East Africa. In some regions it was the norm for young mothers to wear light colours after the birth as well as white pearls around their neck and arms. The cleansing was completed through various magic acts including washing and offering sacrifices, or pouring out a drink-offering for the ancestors. The ancestors were called upon because every new arrival represented a continuation of the tribal line. The ceremonious and festive name-giving, which took place after some days, was usually accompanied by the beating of drums as well as by dancing and singing.

Abbé Demanet described the close relationship between children and adults with great perception: "The mothers love their children tenderly as long as they are small. They never leave them, but carry them around with them always, strapped to their shoulders. They breast-feed them for two years during which time they do not sleep with their husbands. These children grow very quickly partly because of this, but mainly because of the great heat. The girls often reach puberty in their tenth or eleventh year, and the boys just as early ... Once their children are twelve or fifteen days old they carry them around all the time on their backs, as I have already mentioned, and never leave them, no matter what kind of work they are doing. They love them tenderly and try to show to their husband through this tenderness towards the children how devoted they are to him. They continue to show this great care until the children can walk. They then content themselves with feeding them well." (20)

Paul Herman Isert wrote in a letter dated 16 October 1785: "The negroes show an exceptional amount of tenderness towards their children. They never beat them. The mothers may breast-feed them for four years, provided she does not have another child in this period. It is true that the fathers have the right to sell their children, but this happens so rarely that it can hardly be imagined here; and a father, if he has debts and is forced to find money would first try every other possible way before resorting to the sale of his children." (23)

After the third year the exclusive link to the mother was broken by the variety of relations inherent in the extended family. The child learned, by playing with aunts, uncles, grandparents, brothers, sisters and cousins, the complicated rules of social life, respect towards one's elders and the relationship with the older family members. The girls learned to cook the food, went to the market, the boys worked in the fields and acquired some basic handicraft skills. The traditional stories and heroic legends also spoke of bravery and other character virtues. Long before European coloni-

zation, the Koran schools attached to the mosques in the Islamic areas were part of African education. The opportunities for girls to receive an education were severely limited, and only those from top social strata had the chance to learn the basic Arabic script and the sura of the Koran. Women were excluded from the Koran colleges where the future Mula studied, and from such famous theological universities as that in Timbuktu.

Traditional African education was based on the attachment of the child to the community. Alongside the task of acquainting the children with the roots of the ethical, social and spiritual values which formed the basis of communal life, was that of conveying the necessary knowledge required for life in the prevailing conditions. The mother and father in general did not interfere very much, because the children received a good education by playing with other, even older children. The example of the adults had another purpose. The adults were imitated in the simple tasks of everyday life. Example rather than punishment was used in the children's upbringing.

The importance of agricultural and handicraft work was emphasized. Thus children were encouraged to take part in harvest festivals and prayers, in fertility rites and in traditional skills such as that of the smith. The boys learned under the supervision of the fathers and other men all the technical skills necessary for life as it was then. The girls acquired, first through play, later consciously, the farming and household skills of their mothers and the other women. The African writer B. Dadie wrote about the traditional upbringing in the following way: "The children, who at that time did not go to school (except for the Koran and church schools, H. L.), learned the male skills, became farmers, fishers, and the mothers taught them the history of the tribe, which has been forgotten by today's generation. It has been forgotten by a generation which has let itself be lured by the wonders of the West, and ninety percent of whose language consists of foreign words."

It was the custom in many tribes to circumcise the girls at puberty or even before puberty. Olfert Dapper describes the sort of circumcision carried out in West Africa and shows its connection to African religious ideas. "10- or 12-year-old daughters and elder daughters and women were taken to a remote place in the bush not far from the village", and were kept in previously erected huts. A priestess carried out the circumcision and healed the wounds "with green herbs, which sometimes hardly happens within 10 or 12 days. They all stay together for three or four moons and learn dances and songs ..." (10)

The operation could be carried out on various parts. With regard to the technique used in the operation, an attempt was usually made to make the girls as insensitive as possible. Thus among the Masai cold water was thrown over them before the operation. The widespread custom of circumcision was usually performed in connection with coming-of-age or initiation ceremonies, between the age of 10 and 16. These were to mark the transition from childhood to adulthood and were connected with a series of rites and lessons. In Christian Ethiopia circumcision was carried five days after the birth of a girl and seven days after that of a boy.

Circumcision for girls does not necessarily have the same origin as circumcision of boys. With women it was a case of fighting off evil spirits, which presumably prevented fertility. It was also a blood sacrifice, which we will come back to later. The learning that was associated with puberty ceremonies often entailed a sort of test, and was based on practical skills, e.g. managing a household. Sex education and instruction in singing and dancing were also part of it. In the final exam it was often a requirement to prove capability of withstanding pain and torture.

For the banishing of evil spirits and summoning of good spirits the girls stayed in a dense forest or danced under a tree. Virgins who were already promised as brides were often introduced to the secrets of marriage in the place where the ancestors were buried.

In this great importance was attached to the ritual of undressing, standing naked and burning the old clothes, and to giving new names to the girls. Olfert Dapper mentions these elements in his description of the initiation: "As long as they are all together they go about quite naked: for all their clothes are taken by the priestess on their arrival and they never get these clothes back. The older ones who have already been cut can go out and in as often as they like, but they have to leave their clothes outside on the path, and to go to them without clothes. When the time comes for them to be taken out again, a dress is made for them out of bast from trees, which they dye red and yellow, and their friends bring them all sorts of jewellery, bracelets, coral, shells which they put round their legs when they dance and more of the same so that they can adorn themselves when they go out." (10) The final ceremony expresses joy about the "rebirth" of a "new person", who could now take part in conception and birth, and in the further propagation of the ancestral tribe.

The custom of "sewing up" was seldom practised. This custom was used to prevent sex before marriage. In Africa it was only practised among the Galla and Somali, in the East Sudan and in parts of Ethiopia, i.e. in regions which fell under Islamic and Christian influences.

Joseph Ki-Zerbo characterized the position of the African woman—with reference to exactly this point—as follows: "Despite her legally often minor position, despite periodic regressions, when she was looked on as a mobile but inanimate thing, despite polygamy, she was not the beast of burden that she is portrayed as in a certain strand of literature. The African woman was not locked up. She never wore, as far as I know, a chastity belt! Within the matrilinear social structure she had many important rights." (96)

No less important for the thinking of women in old Africa were the fertility ceremonies. Women and men worshipped fertility gods, spirits and demons. Thus the Ibo in West Africa worshipped the goddess Eka-

Abassi as the mother of people and granter of fertility. The goddess Atetie had the same function among the Galla in East Africa. The Masai women (East Africa) celebrated a certain feast in order to pray for fertility. In other tribes the women who wanted a child carried a doll or a similar object on their backs. Prayers were generally said to the ancestors asking them to bless the women with children. Gods, spirits, demons, ancestors—they could all help ensure the line of succession. Among all the peoples of Africa to the south of the Sahara "sacralization" is widespread. Rocks, stones and trees, which stand out because of a particular shape, figures carved in stone or wood which represent people or animals, and also other objects, e.g. stools, drums, screens and vessels are believed to have sacred properties. It was just as common to wear various amulets and talismen. Supernatural, magical powers were attributed to these natural and artificial objects. It was hoped to increase their effect by sacrificial acts (food and drink offerings), for example to raise reproductive power and the ability to conceive. There is nothing greater that African parents can wish for their daughters than a good marriage and numerous offspring in order to ensure the survival and growth of the tribe. This also has a religious aspect. Among the Ashanti (Ghana) a person, as a biological being, inherited the blood of his/her mother and thus acquired status and membership of the extended family, the clan and tribe, through which he learnt his duties. As a spiritual being he was given two things: He got from

71

In contrast to the realistic depictions of animals, representations of humans in rock engravings and drawings were often only in a stylized form. Depiction of a birth.

his father everything which determined his character and person, but his soul, the immortal part, he got directly from a higher being. In Dahomey (Benin) they believed that everybody had at least three souls and that males even had four. One of these was inherited from an ancestor, the second was the individual soul, the third represented the link with the Creator and the fourth in men was related to the concept of fate. It was thought that the ancestor could be born again in one of his/her successors, and that the past repeated itself personified in someone who embodies the character and the deeds of the ancestor. It was also thought that the dead could continue to live either as supernatural beings, sometimes taking on the form of an animal, and sometimes keeping the same external earthly appearance. They could just as easily live on as souls and spirits separated from their bodies. The physical death was not the end of a person. The dead remained members of the tribe; they did not leave the community after death.

Hottentotten an der Mündung des Orange Flusses

72

Family scene. Book illustration. Southern Africa. From: *A Representation of all Lands and Peoples.* Leipzig 1810. Forschungsbibliothek Gotha.

HOME
AND HEARTH

Food gathering and preparation

The division of labour between the sexes was dependent on the degree of economic and cultural progress, and varied according to time and place. Despite the great variation, certain trends can nevertheless be established, especially where the finding and preparation of food are concerned, which were activities very specific to individual African tribes.

The gathering of wild fruits and various roots, herbs and leaves was a task undertaken in primitive societies (and among the bushmen and pygmies right up to the present day) by women. Together with hunting and fishing this provided the economic basis for this early stage in Man's development. In the transition to a class society this role for women retained its importance. Cultivation of the land and the growing of plants remained their task. The transition to a more settled existence and the large-scale cultivation of crops increased the sources of nourishment and increased productivity. It was mainly millet, manioc, ground-nuts and pulses which were cultivated. Often communal land-ownership and cooperative working of the land were what determined social relations among the village-dwellers.

From hunting, men developed animal husbandry. Among the nomad shepherds of the Sahara and in parts of East and South Africa, where women were often kept away from looking after the animals for religious reasons, or at least only had a limited role to play, they were reduced to a position of being a mere "companion" to the man. But there are other examples which show that—for example among the Tuaregs—old matrilinear systems persisted. In other tribes too—for example among the Nama of Namibia—women were involved in looking after the animals, milking the cows and fulfilling other tasks.

Cultivation of the land led to a contrasting socio-economic position of women compared with the nomads, and this was tellingly described by Paul Jacob Bruns at the end of the 18th century. "They grind the rice and millet and make couscous, prepare meals and drinks, spin cotton, make clothes, dye the pagnas, plant corn and tobacco, look after the animals, collect wood, fetch water, sweep out the houses: in short the entire job of maintaining the household is theirs, and when their menfolk are talking among themselves, the women keep off the mosquitoes which would otherwise plague them, and hand them their pipes and tobacco."

The same author says of the daily work-routine of women in South Africa: "The women are very industrious, going early to the forest to cut wood, and when they return home they grind the seed. They till the fields, collect in the harvest, carrying their young in a goatskin on their backs, and stretching their breasts over their shoulder to suckle them as soon as they start to cry." (26)

The traditional domains of men—hunting and fishing—started to be limited by the task of tilling the land. On the other hand, the transition to a market economy created a stimulus for greater integration of the men into agricultural activities.

The tools for tilling the ground were quite simple—often consisting merely of a digging stick or hoe, and work in the fields was time-consuming and exhausting. So the help of all members of the family was needed. The women levelled the ground and broke up the earth with a hoe or a stick. Together with the old people and the young ones, they also sowed the seed, tended the young plants and brought in the harvest. Thus the age-old method of tilling the ground of the Wolof in Senegal is described in *Description of Nigritia* in the late 18th century: "When the rains begin, the negroes, negresses and children leave their huts and go out into the fields; the man carries a sort of hoe, with which he makes a small hole in the ground; the woman follows behind him with a cloth round her body in the form of an apron, in which she has seed which she pours by hand into the hole; behind her is a negro boy or girl, who closes the hole with his or her foot. Thus these three persons advance across the field and sow it with astonishing speed." (24) The men shared the work in the fields, but concentrated on clearing the ground, burning branches and fertilizing the earth with the ash—activities which required greater strength and skill, but were also less time-consuming. In many reports, the work done by the men was valued less highly than that of the hard-working and capable women. In his *History of Loango, Kakongo and other kingdoms in Africa,* Abbé Proyart wrote that the women always worked three days in a row, "the fourth is a rest day, on which they do not have to undertake any work in the fields. The men, who are always resting, work even less on these days." Apart from crop-cultivation, the men carried out other straightforward tasks, they built huts, sometimes helped the women with repair work, and fulfilled their role as warriors. It is thus not true, as sometimes portrayed, that the men lazed around enjoying themselves, while the women were reduced to little more than "work-animals and slaves". Paul Jacob Bruns spoke in these terms of Widah (Dahomey): "Here the men and women work with such industry that they do not rest, once they have started a task, until it is completed. Almost all sorts of corn, beans, yams, and other fruits are planted so close to each other that only a small path is left between them. Even the space around their houses is not left unused, and the inhabitants make as intensive use of their time as they do of space. As soon as they have brought in the harvest, they start sowing again, the land not being left fallow for one instant." (26)

Nevertheless, right into the 19th century and longer, the men, as a rule, did not work for more than seven hours a day. An older man worked about six, a younger one five to seven. Where the women were concerned, things were different. Ethnographers have calculated that a total of about 80% of work in the fields was carried out by women alone. A woman's working day, depending on the season and the nature of the particular work done, could last from sunrise to sunset, i.e. 14 hours, and at other times, too, was seldom less than 9 to 10 hours.

These excessive hours were connected with the large numbers of other activities which had arisen from the natural division of labour between the sexes, and which had persisted. The women had to tend the fire, and fetch water and wood. Much time was also spent on drying fruit, collecting supplies of vegetables, fish and meat. The labours of the women also provided a strong socio-economic support for the matrilinear element in African society, just as religion and tradition, customs and habits all did in the ideological sphere. Nevertheless, over the centuries, depending on which tribe and which region was concerned, male influence continued to make progress, firstly in the towns, but gradually also in the country. Patrilinear influences which began among the nomadic shepherds, spread increasingly among the farmers as well. Animal husbandry also played an important role. From the combining of crop-cultivation (female) and animal-rearing (male) there developed, in some parts of Africa (Sudan and Ethiopia), field cultivation using draught animals and ploughs. Men, by taking control of the extended family's possessions, gained more and more privileges, supported by urbanization and Islam and Christianity, while women slid more and more into a subservient role. It has already been stressed on a number of occasions that this development was not an even one, and women in some rural areas have retained many rights up to the present day. In the development of new sources of food, and the preparation of food, more and more separate and complex areas emerged and more and more specialist duties for women developed.

Culinary skills were also an "invention" of women. In developing these, women established an important basis for forming families. Over the centuries, specific customs relating the food and eating and drinking developed. The basic diet of the nomadic shepherds consisted of meat soups and milk products, that of the cultivators, of plant products. In Johann Leo one reads: "The common people customarily eat meat twice a week. The more wealthy eat it every day, according to taste, and have three meals per day." On the whole, the peasants had one warm meal a day, usually at midday or in the evening. The rest of the time they made do with leftovers, washed down with millet-beer. To save time and effort, the women of one extended family often cooked together at one hearth, supervised by the oldest woman. P. Antonio Zucchelli from Gradisca wrote of his experiences in the Congo: "These blacks, however wealthy or refined they are, still only eat one cooked meal a day, and if anyone wishes to eat something in the evening, then he eats raw things and fruit." (15)

The eating habits and the methods of preparing food and drink of the upper social classes which emerged, for example, in the course of "Islamization" in West Africa, developed differently from those of the common people. The Englishman, John Matthew, wrote of Sierra Leone in the years 1785–87: "Men and women always take their meals separately and drink only water with their food. During the day they only eat twice, once at 10 in the morning and once at sundown. The more wealthy, however, have a light meal in the early morning, which the wife who slept with the man the previous night has to prepare." (21)

Although the quality of the food eaten by the majority of the population left a lot to be desired, and there was little variety, the preparation of food, a task undertaken by the women, was a lengthy process. Hour-long grinding of maize for flour, and the brewing of beer both were important tasks. In the *Description of Nigritia*, a report about Senegal dating from the late 18th century, one can read that the main food was couscous. "It is almost incredible how much work is involved in the preparation of this food, which looks and tastes so simple." Couscous, coscus or kuskus, was an easily digested and refreshing millet mash, from which dumplings were made, which were served with hot soup. In Senegal this was accompanied by palm wine, a sort of beer made from boiled and fermented maize sweetened with fruit. In Sierra Leone the staple diet was rice, with palm-oil or a rich meat soup with much pepper, spices, and palm. Meat itself was a rarity. In West Africa, pigs, sheep, goats, oxen, hens, and also ducks were eaten. According to Mungo Park's (1795-1797) description, "free people" breakfasted "at daybreak usually on a mash made of flour and water given a sour flavour with tamarind. At 2 in the afternoon, usually a flour-paste with milk and some tree-butter is eaten; but the main meal of the day is the evening one, which is seldom ready before midnight. It usually consists of couscous, with a little meat or tree-butter added." (30)

In a *History of Dahomey* (1799), which Archibald Dalzel put together during a stay in Africa of many years, one finds the following about the natives' culinary arts: "They have few dishes, but these are excellent. Among them the best is black soup, which is made either of meat or fish with various plants, heavily seasoned with pepper and salt and with palm-oil added … Their bread is made of maize or millet sometimes cooked to a stiff pudding and sometimes baked with or without sour dough. They also make a light, white, slightly fermented bread …" (66)

Women sometimes became prisoners of their own inventions, but also sometimes raised them to the level of a profession which went beyond the bounds of the family—as is shown, for example, by cooking. At an early stage, sources mention "professional" cooking and carrying of water as a specialized task of women. In Ethiopia "cooks with coarse aprons prepare the meals and bring them on earthenware platters into the eating area. The platters are on great round flat wooden trays which they carry on their heads. They have straw lids of various colours." In Abomey, Dahomey, the town's population was supplied with water from a distant stream: "This commodity is thus at a premium and there are a number of women whose job is to carry it round the town in earthenware vessels and sell it."

It can be assumed that such specialized cooking and water-carrying was a development which took place largely in the towns.

Craft-work activities

The original craft-work activities centred round pottery and weaving or plaiting. The natural environment—earth and forest—supplied the raw materials with which objects for domestic use were manufactured. Vessels were made of clay, baskets from twigs, mats and ropes from fibres.

The old reports always stress the great variety of work undertaken by women. Thus Paul Jacob Bruns writes of South Africa: "They make earthenware vessels with the same skill as the men. The baskets and sleeping-mats are the work of women. Baskets are made of grasses woven so tightly that they will hold any liquid." (26)

Literary sources constantly mention a number of typical female activities in towns and in the rural areas: gathering, cultivating crops, making pots, preparing food and drink, selling goods in the market,

73

By the role they played in the world of work, women were able to assert their rights. Threshing. Book illustration. Madagascar. From: *General History of Voyages by Land and Sea ...*, Leipzig 1747. Forschungsbibliothek Gotha.

building dwellings, making cloth, but also fishing and weaving. African women—just as their counterparts in other parts of the world—played an important role in the material culture of the time. The sources do not always reveal whether the articles they produced were for domestic use or for the market. As the natural economy—production for one's own use—predominated, both rural peasants and town-dwellers produced their own textiles and clothing. In the towns, the wives and children of craftsmen often grew food on the outskirts of the town.

Women were also responsible for the development of pottery. They made clay imitations of the containers made from gourds which were used for water, and let them dry in the sun. They soon discovered that if they put these containers over a fire the clay hardened further. Later, too, pottery was largely a female occupation, while the men, if they practised it at all, usually made tobacco-pipes. The introduction of the mortar for grinding the corn was also a female invention of that time.

The idea of making baskets for carrying things probably emerged among the collectors and gatherers. The art of weaving was then transferred from baskets to mats and other objects. The weaving of cloth developed. The preparation of plant and animal fibres for spinning, and the spinning of the thread itself, was usually a female task. The original introduction of the weaving of cloth was very probably a female achievement, even though it was men who developed it and invented the loom, usually men, often older ones, who produced cloth and made this into garments. European travellers in West Africa reported that indigo and cotton grew there, and cloth was produced, largely by women, which was dyed in various colours. "Cotton which may only be gathered in the fields, where it grows on its own, is spun by the women, and the men make cloth from it which they then sell, if they do not use it themselves ..." (24) Women were hardly at all involved in making garments. They produced calico which consisted of several strips. "When

they have made a suitable number of such strips," wrote Abbé Demanet, "they sew them together according to the use they wish to make of them; only seldom do they cut them." H. C. Monrad makes the remark that in some parts of West Africa "women concern themselves with spinning and weaving, using a small hand-spindle which they move up and down, and even walk around with." Mungo Park reported that among the Mandingo—with the exception of weaving—all work, the preparation of the cotton, the spinning, dyeing, and sewing was carried out by the women. On the slave-coast "the women spin and card the cotton and the men weave and sew", according to Paul Jacob Bruns. He also mentions itinerant male craftsmen who travelled around with their looms, which were short, light and portable. On Madagascar, on the other hand, it was women who did the weaving. "For weaving only women are used, because the work is regarded as unworthy of men", the same traveller reported.

The dyeing of cloth has already been mentioned. The colours ranged from red, black and green to yellow; it is also mentioned that cloth was "left quite white".

Among the country dwellers, the women also played an important role in the building of the huts from wattle and daub, while the wives of the nomadic shepherds, in addition to their time-consuming domestic chores, not only had to provide the material for their shelters, but also were responsible for finding new areas on which to erect them, for transporting them from one place to another and also were laden with the milk-carriers, straw mats and pots. "The tents are made of material made from goat and camel hair, which is so dense that rainwater seldom penetrates it", writes Paul Jacob Bruns. "This material is prepared by the women, who also carry out all other domestic functions. They brush the horses, gather wood, fetch water, bake bread, cook meals etc." (26)

Everything to do with decorative ornaments, for example the weaving of all conceivable domestic objects, the making of jewellery from glass beads and plants or the soft material made of raffia by the Bakuba, was the work of women. In some tribes woven mats were used to decorate the houses. The huts were covered in them, one hung near the entrance, the rooms were divided off and the floor covered with them. Geometric designs and colourful patterns were woven into them. Some pots and pans and wooden bowls of various sizes, a few other objects, and mats for sleeping on, were all that most people in West Africa possessed. The wealthier also had magnificent chests, beautiful carpets, lamps and other luxury articles. Clapperton wrote of Bornu: "The people have few household objects—a few earthenware pots for cooking, very prettily made, and wooden bowls. Water, their only beverage, is kept cool in earthenware jugs and drunk out of large calabashes." These domestic objects were manufactured with much care and tasteful imagination.

In Mauritania, leather goods—cushions, bags, corn sacks, with a scratched decoration, bright embroidery or applique work—were produced. Beautifully made boxes were used to contain tools and other objects. First they were decorated with leather, later with perforated copper plates whose value was enhanced even more by the addition of finely chased silver.

The lifestyle of women depended very much on whether they lived in an urban area or on the land. Above all, the higher degree of division of labour in the towns was significant. The chances of a woman carrying out craftwork or selling in the market were greater here. An investigation of life in the kingdom of Benin carried out by the African historian Dike allows us to state that before the appearance of the Portuguese, the town was surrounded by hundreds of villages in which all kinds of folk-art flourished: weaving, pottery and metal-work. The urban environment also offered more opportunities for the education of children than the rural one.

Trading developed early on, and a more or less continuous exchange of goods took place on market-places in towns and on the land. This was essentially a

N° 38.

Frauensperfonen von Kazegut in verfchiedener Kleidung.

74

Women's clothing from West Africa. Book illustration. From: *General History of Voyages by Land and Sea...*, Leipzig 1747. Forschungsbibliothek Gotha.

male domain, and they often had to transport the goods which they offered for exchange for miles by land or by river. But women also secured a role for themselves, even though this was usually confined to the local market. They sold specially-prepared foods and pottery. Where they brewed beer they set up little sales points. Connected with this may be the fact that one of the oldest professions for women in towns was prostitution.

Their "natural" domains, as evolved from the original division of labour, led to men and women carrying out activities which developed into specialized skills which were often passed on from one generation to the next. And it may come as a surprise to learn that women's share in this development originally predominated—apart from the (revolutionary) area of metal-working, which was dominated by men from the start, and woodcarving, where women only served as assistants to men.

The art of woodcarving—the most widespread craft in Africa to the south of the Sahara—developed from the need to manufacture such domestic artefacts as beds, stools, drums, bowls, jugs, pipes and many others.

All these objects were made from one piece of wood. Ornamentation was usually representational. Carved beds and chairs were a privilege of the wealthy. To reduce the weight of large carved objects (for example, beds, which could be up to two metres long) the ornamented side-panels were cut through, and small human figures or totem animals (for example panthers, buffaloes, elephants, crocodiles, baboons, lizards, chameleons, snakes, tortoises, toads and spiders) carved out. The headboard also often consisted of an animal shape.

A stool carved out of a single piece of wood took the form of a cylinder. The round base and the seat were linked by a sculpture which either encased a hollow interior or formed a pedestal. Sometimes it was provided with a back consisting of one or two human figures—if two, then a man and a woman.

75

Fulbe girl in ceremonial costume.

In metalworking, women were used as assistants. In some places they even had an important role to play in the extraction of the raw materials.

In West Africa there were, from the earliest times, reports of female gold-panners. Of panning in the gold-mines of the Dutch and English trading settlements on the west coast we read that "the law and their religion only allowed women, and then only for six weeks in the year, to work in these, and they did so in the following manner: These women have no other tools for extracting the gold from the ground than two or three wooden pans filled with water. Into these they put three or four feet of earth from the mines, so that the pans are about half filled; they add water to this and rub the earth with all their strength, tipping the pan so, that the water pours away with the earth; this operation they repeat until nothing remains on the bottom of the pan but fragments of gold, which they collect and carry home in the evening." (24)

These women only made limited profit from these activities in the 17th and 18th centuries, and remained dependent on men. "Even if a woman is very industrious and earns a lot from gold-panning and suchlike, the man allows her no more luxury than the other women, and she can make no other use of the fortune she has amassed than to live better with her children." (24)

Work and formal dress, jewellery, body care

The high degree of craftsmanship, in the development of which women played such an important role, was found also in clothes and jewellery. One of the oldest reports about the outward appearance of African women can be found in *Johann Leo the African's Description of Africa*, dating from the year 1526, which, however, deals more with Islamized women. A traveller's account of 1609 about the island of Madagascar gives an equally interesting picture: "The women on this island have short hair, like the men, their jewellery consists of arm bangles made of tin or silver and round balls. Their clothing is woven and reaches down to their knees. They also wear sleeveless vests over their breasts." (8)

It is worth mentioning here the cotton pagnas which the women wore round their waists. Abbé Demanet reports of these: "One of these garments, which reach down to their calves and beyond, serves instead of a skirt or stockings. On feast days they throw another over their shoulders and fold it back over their heads. They are thus clothed from head to foot ... Nothing is more colourful than this apparel, to which they add arm bangles, an enormous belt made of fragments of glass, neck-cloths and earrings. They carefully apply palm-oil to their hair."

Clothes and styles of dressing throughout the world are closely linked with the development of distinct historical and ethnographic areas, each with its own material and spiritual culture. Women's clothing, like that of men, developed out of the need both for protection and for decoration. Covering the body protected it from heat and cold, but also from magical forces and evil spirits. The actual form taken by the clothing depended largely on climate, sex, age and the specific purpose for which it was required.

A clear differentiation was made in clothing, and also in additional jewellery, between everyday apparel and that for special occasions such as feasts or ceremonies.

Female clothing could be seamless or sewn, enveloping, covering or decorating. Africa produced a rich variety of artistic forms of decoration for their clothing or their bodies. It had an aesthetic, but often also a magic function. "Magic medicine", kept in special, highly decorated containers, was commonplace, and this included small, exquisitely made pendants in the form of animals, which were worn as talismen or amulets. Rings or little decorative objects like drums or axes were supposed to prolong one's life. Little masks which people carried everywhere with them were supposed to guard against danger. Other fetishes, of which, travellers' reports tell us, there were many, also served as ornaments. Clothing and jewellery served in combination as an outward marker of social status. Earrings and spiral wire bangles worn on arms and legs could, when they were worn by the rich and were made of gold, weigh 20 pounds or more. Upper class ladies willingly made certain sacrifices in order to display their wealth.

The Italian missionary, P. Antonio Zucchelli from Gradisca, in his *Extraordinary Description of a Missionary Journey to Congo in Ethiopia*, published in 1715, gives a description, in the customarily pious language of the time, of how the "heathen women" satisfy their vanity with rich jewellery: "Round their necks several hollow brass chains", on their feet particularly thick ones which hindered them in walking. In neighbouring areas the women "in order to appear neater and more attractive" wore "many glass bangles on their legs." In addition, women had themselves tattooed all over, "all sorts of figures in curious shapes carved into the living flesh, into their breasts, stomachs, shoulders." (15) (The word *tattoo* is derived from the Tahitian word *tatau*, whose actual meaning is to draw correctly, accurately. With the discovery of the Polynesian islands in the 18th century this word entered European languages as the name given to a certain method of decorating the body.) Throughout Africa in general, incisions in the flesh—scar tattooing—was common. Men and women decorated their bodies by burning or by cutting patterns or by inserting dyes; the significance of this varies greatly.

On Madagascar wealthy women wore arm bangles made of copper or silver, earrings made of gold, long neck-chains, with different sorts of decorations such as toothpicks, pendants etc. The British ship's officer, John Matthew, tells us about the outward appearance of women in Sierra Leone, which he visited from 1785 to 1787. "They wear bracelets and necklets made of coral, silver rings, chains and manillas (which are flat or rounded silver rings round their wrists). They also

76

The progressing division of labour and the use of new methods of work aimed at a high productivity increased social differences, but also offered the possibility for trades and professions to develop. Women of various social origins: women of high status, simple women, slaves. From: *General History of Voyages by Land and Sea ...*, Leipzig 1747. Forschungsbibliothek Gotha.

use make-up, of which they have various kinds. In their ears they wear gold earrings and round their necks a string of large pieces of coral and a gold or silver chain with a locket, on each wrist two or three manillas, from each of which hang five or six silver rings." (21)

The Danish preacher H. C. Monrad, who visited West Africa from 1805 to 1809, described "keys" of silver, gold and brass, which were finely made and worn by women. Europeans took such jewellery home with them as souvenirs. Rich women wore so much gold jewellery that they could barely walk. In Timbuktu the American, James Riley, met women who were bedecked with gold ornaments, pearls, shells, ear and nose rings, bracelets on their arms and in their hair. He described how he exchanged a small box filled with snuff for the gold jewellery of an African woman; it weighed more than a pound. The traveller brought this valuable jewellery back to the USA as a present for his wife.

Bracelets for arms and legs, and, in particular, strings of glass beads, had a musical effect, for every movement set them jangling and tinkling. "A fashionably dressed woman is supposed to wear 8 to 10 talers attached to silver chains hanging from each hip, so that they rattle and tinkle when she walks; she also should wear silver spurs on her feet, and have many keys at her side, even if she only has one casket which is secured by a lock,"—thus Ludewig Ferdinand Römer, on the coast of Guinea. (18)

The French commandant of Fort Saint Louis in Senegal described similarly adorned women: "One main decoration which they use consists of ten or twelve strings of the finest pieces of glass, which they wear round their loins, concealed, their presence only betrayed by the noise when they walk. On their feet they wear sandals and gold or silver foot-chains; on their hands a sort of golden bracelet, if they can afford it; in their ears they wear the heaviest earrings possible, which are tied to the head with a thread, to prevent them tearing the ear-lobe."

MÄNNER UND WEIBER DER HOTTENTOTTEN
nach den leben gezeichnet.

77

Men and women. Book illustration. Southern Africa. From: *General History of Voyages by Land and Sea …*, Leipzig 1747. Forschungsbibliothek Gotha.

The descriptions point to there being a link between clothing and jewellery on the one hand, and the position of the woman within the family, on the other. It was customary for the young unmarried women to cover their bodies with fewer clothes than the married ones. "The young unmarried daughters of the chiefs between the age of 12 and 16 wear a dac, which is made of the largest bits of coral which exist, and nut-sized pieces of gold and silver which are strung together with a strong cotton thread. This dac, which is worn round the neck and over the shoulders and hangs down at the back and front, where it is crossed, is all the ornament they wear, except when they put something round their loins which hangs to half-way down their thighs. The rest of their body is uncovered in order not to hide its beauty." (24)

The above-mentioned James Riley wrote of the west coast and the interior of Africa: "The married women wear on their heads a kind of cap made of blue material or silk, and cotton cloths of various types and colours." (35)

In some areas of Africa south of the Sahara, in particular the equatorial regions and the Congo, women's clothing was described as "scant and simple". The simple African woman, for her daily tasks, often wore very little at all. But, even where the climate was such that little was worn, a difference was made between everyday clothing and that worn on special occasions. It is also true to say that covering up the bosom was not introduced by the African women but rather, where it did, later on, occur, was the result of outside influences. Despite various prejudices about alleged "nakedness" which are found in early reports, these also emphasized that the women, despite their scanty clothing, had a sense of propriety and lived modest and pure lives. Only a complete ignorance of the history of ethnography in general and of Africa in particular, could have led to associating such behaviour with "lack of chastity". Nowhere in the world did clothing develop from a feeling of modesty, but rather the feeling of modesty or immodesty came from the wearing of clothes. It should be remembered that, until not so very long ago, prejudices originating in Christian ideas demanded the covering of the legs and arms of European women. It is a fact that morality in other parts of the world, which had its roots in the totality of the particular socio-economic development and the interrelationships and mutual influences of the local population, knew no compulsion to cover up the body. In the same way there were no "commandments" as are typical for European cultures.

In most parts of Africa it was customary to paint the body, and this had special significance, probably linked with tribal allegiances, and was carried out as part of initiation, marriage and death rites. The custom probably dated back to earliest times, and perhaps expressed blood-relationships, divisions into exogamous groups, or some sort of protective magic.

In some places, the custom persisted until recent times of boys and girls daubing their bodies with white clay after the initiation rites, warriors and girls painting their bodies red for festive occasions, or nursing mothers putting a mark in white clay on their foreheads. Oskar Lenz reported in 1877 of the Ogowe tribes in West Africa: "A widespread custom consists of painting the face and arms white or yellow and red to mark special occasions such as funerary rites, dances, wars etc." (44) Tattooing, mentioned above, was also used in this context.

Body care compared very favourably with what was customary in Europe at the time. A thorough daily wash or, where possible, bathing in the open air, were the norm.

For skin-care, ointments made of oil, red and yellow powder and other ingredients were used in order to achieve a fine, soft, black, gleaming skin. The Bakuba (Congo basin) had finely-decorated wooden boxes in which redwood was crumbled and mixed together with water or palm-oil. On special occasions this mixture was applied to the body.

In all regions much time was spent on the hair. Dyes were known, too. We read in the *History of Lo-*

ango, *Kakongo and other kingdoms in Africa* by the French missionary, Abbé Proyart: "The heads of those wishing to distinguish themselves by their charm are like flower-gardens: one can see oaths and figures of all sorts drawn on them."

It was reported of Madagascan ladies that they could spend up to an entire day preparing their hair or having it prepared by someone else. It goes without saying that the ever more time-consuming preparation of women's hair particularly in the towns led early on to the development of a specialization by certain women, who were in this way early precursors of today's hairdressers.

In Africa, clothing and jewellery reflected a process which lasted for thousands of years and remained relatively stable from primitive society, through the early class societies, right down to the present day. They expressed the aesthetic ideas of their creators and wearers. Alone the different forms which the ornaments and jewellery took are proof of the rich imagination and inventiveness of the women, and the long traditions on which they could draw. And, not least, the need to decorate themselves was, in itself, an expression of joyous vitality.

Healing

What was the role of women in healing and medicine? Here, too, they were active in a wide area, and their activities often verged on a professional role. Women played a significant role not just in the material culture, housing, food, domestic matters, clothing and jewellery, but also in the spiritual and intellectual culture, as is shown by their involvement in healing. This was, of course, again connected with the natural division of labour, but also with the role of women as preservers of tradition, customs and beliefs, a role which will be discussed in the sections on religious cults and art.

In addition to animal products it was plants, herbs and fruits which made up the main elements in African medicaments, and these were collected for centuries by women. Included here should also be honey, which played an important role in the treatment of the sick. The very earliest sources speak of a whole spectrum of medicaments and healing methods, powders, decoctions, poultices and embrocations. The most important method, blood-letting, was applied in the same way for century after century. Water was a tradition element, for external use, as a drink for internal complaints or for washing for protection from magic powers. Women were involved in helping with births, female complaints and cosmetic treatments. The "medicine men", who had a comprehensive knowledge of local healing plants, juices, fruits, roots and leaves, often could not have managed without the aid of women. Selected women were often called in to help diagnose sudden illnesses. Among the Mende in West Africa there were oracle statues which stood in the house of a women's secret society dedicated to healing. If such a statue was to be consulted it first had the society's medicine rubbed into it and was then held out at arms' length by the leader of the society so that she was looking directly in its face. The statue answered questions about the causes of the illness and the probable fate of the victim by nodding. In 1877 Oskar Lenz in his *Sketches from West Africa* wrote: "Even the women play a role among the Ogowe inasmuch as it is they who have medicine and pharmacy in their hands. If a villager falls ill the women go into the forest in order to discuss the case—what they say and do there nobody knows, for men are strictly excluded from these gatherings. When they return they are able to say whether the sick person will recover or will die." (44)

Folk medicine and healing methods had two aspects in old Africa: on the one hand they were magic practices, on the other they were products of real experience. In the gentile society reality could not be separated from the supernatural world, and magic could not be separated from experience; both formed an indivisible whole—with both medically harmful and also useful elements. This resulted from the dialectics of the "magic view of the world" which conditioned the largely rural population over the centuries.

In Africa the ghosts of ancestors, malign magicians, the ghosts of sickness, but also natural forces, impurity and natural causes were regarded as being responsible for illness. Magic as often practised by healers had its roots in religious beliefs. Surgery, too, had a long tradition in Africa. As long as three thousand years ago, successful brain operations were carried out. But women seem to have been only the objects of major operations. Even Caesarean births, in which the child was surgically removed from the mother's body in order to save the life of mother and child, were known in Africa long before the first contacts with Europeans. The traveller Felkin writes that he witnessed such an operation in Uganda in 1879. He described the Caesarean operation on a young 20-year-old who was having her first child. "During the application of the needles the patient gave not a single cry, and an hour after it was over she seemed quite well ... two hours after the operation she was able to suckle the child. On the third morning the wound was stitched and some of the needles were removed, the rest on the fifth and sixth days. The wound oozed strange liquids which were removed with a sponge. By the eleventh day the wound had healed." (121) It is probable that such an operation was a relative rarity in Africa.

Women's professional involvement in medicine seems to have started with midwifery, which was probably, together with the collecting of healing plants, the oldest activity of African women. There were women midwives, and it was women who were often responsible for circumcision of the children. In some parts of Africa (e.g. in Ethiopia), the mothers undertook the operation with a sharp knife; or in other cases professional or part-time midwives did it. Among the Ewe in West Africa it used to be mothers solely who helped their daughters in childbirth. Among the Masai and the Swaheli, however, it is reported that there were women who were professional midwives and were paid for their pains.

Birth was made easier by various rites. The Masai midwives examined pregnant women during the last months of pregnancy and tried, by massage, to put the unborn child in the best position for birth. In other tribes massage was also used, together with other measures. In addition there were special rules on diet. There were many therapies for complaints during pregnancy. After the birth the midwife cleaned the newborn child and started it breathing. Palm-kernel oil and redwood were used for baby-care, also powder mixed with lavender. Among the Lunda the woman drank a decoction of a root, after the birth, in order to prevent prolonged bleeding. The nursing mother was given special body care. For the entire time she was breast-feeding the child, diet continued to play an important role.

Every clay vessel had
characteristic ornaments.
Clay vessel of the Mang-
betu, Zaïre. Height 41 cm.
Museum für Völker-
kunde, Frankfurt/Main.

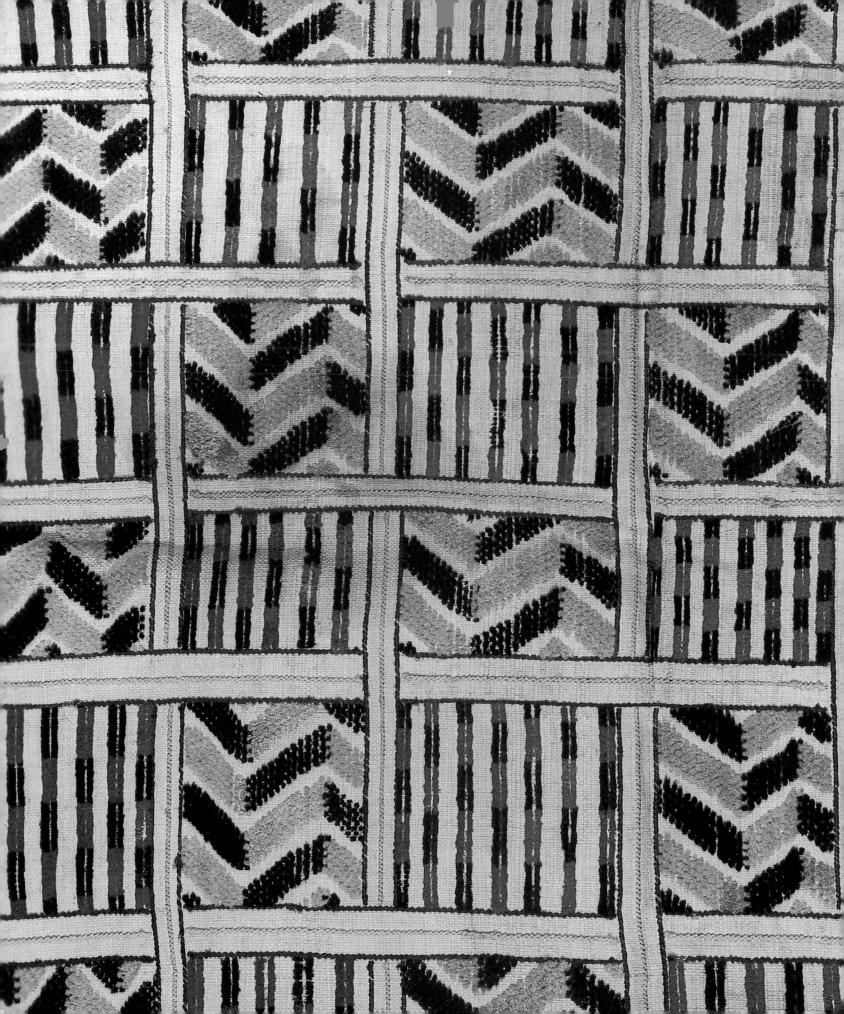

79

These velvety materials from the Kuba of the Congo were used both for clothing and also for decorative purposes. Museum für Völkerkunde, Leipzig.

80

Mother with child. Height 100 cm. Cameroon. Staatliches Museum für Völkerkunde, Linden-Museum, Stuttgart.

81

The bottle-shaped vessel from the region to the north of the Congo estuary has burned patterns and incrustations with white earth. Height 19 cm. Museum für Völkerkunde, Leipzig.

82

Carved gourd vessel. Yoruba, Nigeria. Museum für Völkerkunde, Hamburg.

83

Clay pot, around 1900. Height 16 cm. South Africa. Museum für Völkerkunde, Dresden.

84

Spoons were prestige
objects and were only
used on special occasions.
Large spoons with a
carved head as a handle
were often signs of a
high-ranking wife of a
chief. Wood. Rauten-
strauch-Joest-Museum,
Cologne.

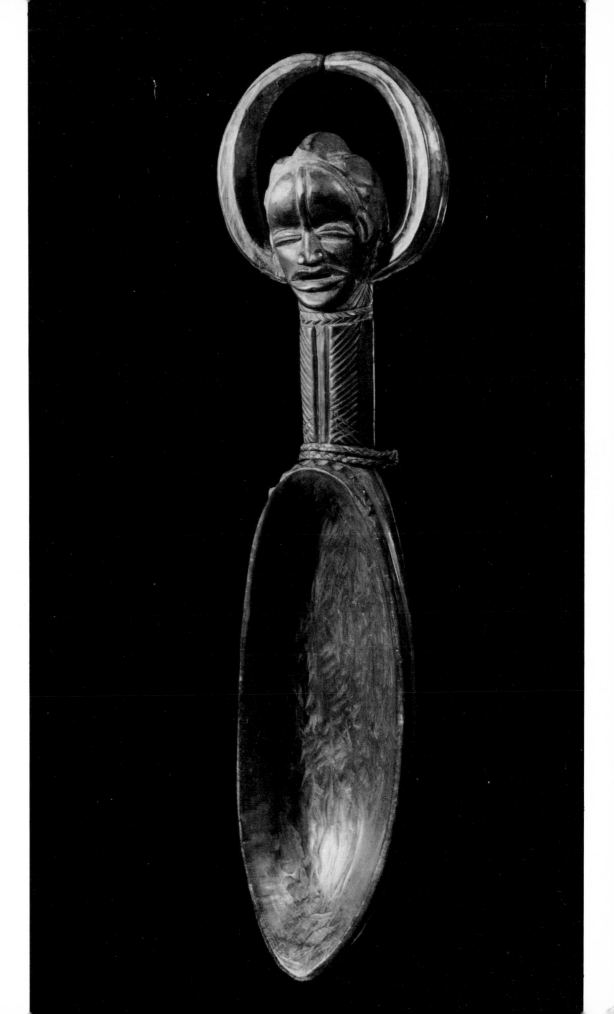

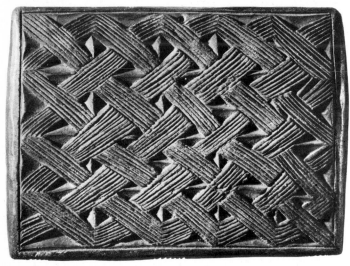

87

Women had the task of decorating the living quarters. Box for storing gold dust. Brass. Ghana. Museum für Völkerkunde, Staatliche Museen Preussischer Kulturbesitz, Berlin (West).

85/86

These ornamental lids from Nupe served earlier as book-covers and later as mirror frames. Length 19 cm, width 13.5 cm. Museum für Völkerkunde, Leipzig.

88

This type of vessel was displayed for decorative purposes in people's houses. Carved gourd. Yoruba, Nigeria. Museum für Völkerkunde, Hamburg.

Eine Hottentottin.

89

Woman with child in her arms, riding on an ox. Book illustration. Southern Africa. From: *General History of Voyages by Land and Sea …*, Leipzig 1747. Forschungsbibliothek Gotha.

90

Ethiopian women in traditional ceremonial costume.

91

Clay vessel. Mangbetu, Zaïre. Tropical Museum, Amsterdam.

92

Women showed great skill in making all craft-objects. Calabash. Rautenstrauch-Joest-Museum, Cologne.

93

In the Kikuya region of Kenya, women work in the banana plantations. Bananas are an important source of nourishment, and are boiled, fried, dried, mashed and made into wine.

94

The skills and techniques of pottery are handed down from generation to generation. Ethiopia.

95

In rural areas women work on the land for no less than nine to ten hours a day, depending on the season and the work to be done. Young woman pounding maize. Ovambo, Southwest Africa.

96

Burdens are traditionally carried on their heads. Wood-carrier. Bamum, Cameroon.

97

In many areas African women used weaving-looms. Bowl with woman at loom. Wood. North Yoruba, Nigeria. Museum für Völkerkunde, Staatliche Museen Preussischer Kulturbesitz, Berlin (West).

98

Just as they did centuries ago, women in groups thread fish-bones together to make chains. Kenya.

99

Cloth made from plant fibres, goat and camel hair is used for domestic purposes and also sold. Production of a dress from banana fibres. Ethiopia.

100

Skills associated with women right up to the present day were spinning, sewing and dyeing. Woman spinning cotton. Galla, Ethiopia.

101

Women decorated cushions, bags, shoes and sandals with paintwork, embossing, appliqué and embroidery work. Objects were often decorated with geometrical patterns. Cushion cover. Leather with coloured cloth and leather appliqué work. 53 × 63 cm. Republic of Dahomey. Museum für Völkerkunde, Leipzig.

102

Make-up box made of a turtle-shell decorated with iron and glass beads, around 1900. Length 16.5 cm, bredth 11 cm. Southwest Africa (Namibia), Herero. Museum für Völkerkunde, Dresden.

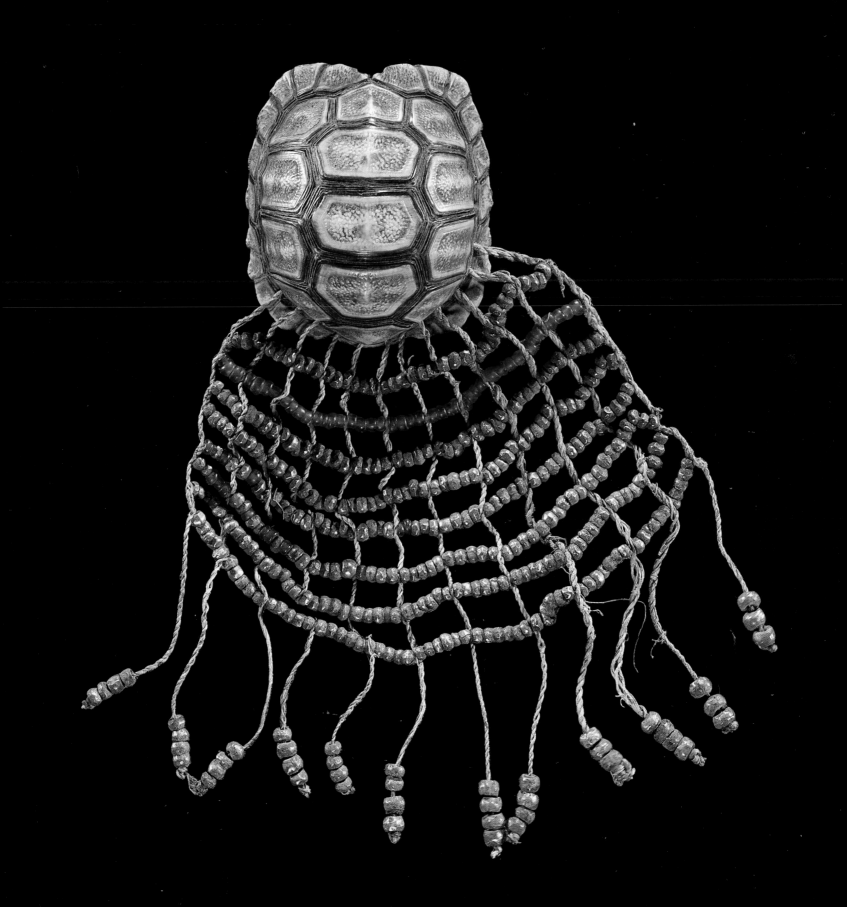

WOMEN AND RELIGIOUS CULTS

Religious cults had an enormous influence on the development of the intellectual and, partly also, the material culture of the African kingdoms. They formed an integral part of the spiritual and intellectual culture of the African peoples and had a considerable influence on their lifestyle and on the relationship between men and women.

The main elements in tribal religions were magic and fetishism, i.e. the worship of various inanimate objects. Other essential elements were animism, the belief in the spiritual nature of all things, forces and natural phenomena, and ancestor-worship. Ancestors were represented as statues or masks and were offered prayers and sacrifices. Life in Africa was—with some exaggeration—described as taking place "in the sign of one's ancestors". When polytheistic state religions developed in the kingdoms, these took over many elements of the old tribal beliefs. From the ghosts of the ancestors developed the gods, who had more specific functions, personal names, and a wider area of activity. Like a sort of hereditary aristocracy, the gods were linked by close relations and were dominated by leaders. As already mentioned, peoples with a highly developed state system raised earthly kings into the ranks of the gods, and declared their ancestors also to have been gods. Kings and queens were thus protected from excessive contact with their fellow human beings by various taboos, laws and superstitions.

Priestesses were active in various central holy places. In addition to the "house of ancestors" which the non-itinerant peasants set up in their villages, buildings were erected in West Africa and other regions which the old travellers' accounts compare with temples. The Ibo (Nigeria) constructed such temples, to the honour of the earth goddess Ala, in quiet corners of the woods away from any settlements. The roof, a pitched roof made of straw, on a stepped base, was covered with clay sculptures representing the gods, men and animals. Those of men and animals were life-sized. In the centre of the pillared area was the figure of the goddess Ala with a child on her knee—the motif of mother and child was widespread in the representational art of the African peoples. The clay pillars were decorated with reliefs and paintings. A close synthesis of geometrical forms, scenic representations, reliefs and sculptures was achieved. These buildings were the domain of priestesses, soothsayers, oracles and healers, which Ludewig Ferdinand Römer, in his *News from the Coast of Guinea* refers to repeatedly as "fetish-women". The concept of "fetish" has already been mentioned. Every object received mystical powers of differing natures from a god. Particularly powerful were fetishes which were housed in the villages or at the side of the road in special huts: bundles of leaves, bones, feathers, horns, animal hairs or claws, a large rounded stone, living or stuffed animals. Like fetishes, magic was an attribute of the "real medicine man" and priest, means by which the peasants and nomadic shepherds, with their as yet scanty knowledge of nature, tried to base their relationship with their environment. Paul Herman Isert, in his *Voyage to Guinea and the Caribbean Islands in Columbia* describes, in a letter of 28th March 1785, temples in West Africa, more than thirty of them in one spot, in which women gave lessons to children. "I saw some which had many fore-courts and various rooms, and were surrounded with the most beautiful flowers ... Each temple has its school, in which the priestesses give the children lessons in singing and dancing." (23)

It was not by chance that it was women who were giving the following generations instruction in customs and traditions, for example marriage norms, explaining the genealogy of the tribe, its descent from its ancestors, often a tribal mother, and giving basic instruction in physical, arithmetic and medicinal knowledge, aesthetic ideas as well as in poetic and musical creativity.

In West Africa it was not just the long-preserved islands of matrilinearity but also the bilateral lines of relationship and inheritance which were mirrored in female or mixed orders of priesthood, as Brodie Cruickshank reported in *Eighteen years on the African Gold Coast.* In Ghana in the middle of the 19th century there were, according to Cruickshank, priests and priestesses, and the latter were on the increase. Priesthood was "not confined to the male part of the population; rather there is also an order of priestesses or fetish-women, and the ranks of these religious harpies are constantly on the increase", wrote the English traveller. "Their role is little different to that of the men, with whom they preside over most religious ceremonies; their most important function is within the processions and dances in honour of the fetish, to which they lend life and excitement by their singular dress, wild gestures, shrill cries and demented behaviour." (43)

Religious cults formed the basis for emancipatory movements, particularly in deviation from official dogmas, the heresies of the great religions, above all Christianity, in Africa south of the Sahara. Characteristic for Christianity, in addition to its widespread nature, transcending political and ethnic frontiers, were the dominating patrilinear elements. Thus early opposition to Christianity in the Congo combined the interests of the lower social strata with those of women.

One example was the prophet movement under the clever leadership of Vita Kimba, in the kingdom of Congo. Towards the end of the 17th century there formed among the Christians in the Congo, a popular movement which derived its inspiration from the Mother of God and prophesied a Last Judgement of God. Its supporters were called after Saint Anthony. From 1703–1706 it was led by the twenty-year-old Vita Kimba. Originally a priestess in an African temple, she had been baptized into the Christian faith under the name of Donna Béatrice. Then she believed she had been called upon to become a prophet, claiming to have died and to have been reincarnated as a man, Saint Anthony. As in the case of the African queen, Nzinga Mbande, she desired to play a male role. To her supporters she appeared as a robed priest complete with Christian halo, as was central to the ritual of the traditional African religions. Her power was based on her own total belief in her reincarnation as Saint Anthony.

She had a temple built on the site of the former bishopric and formed a group of disciples who travelled the land preaching the word. Vita Kimba's teaching was that Christ came into the world as an African, and that his apostles were black. She planned a national church which would be independent of Rome but would be nevertheless Christian, and she wished to achieve an "Africanization" of the Christian message in which what were regarded as "heathen excesses" (initiation rites, polygamy, presents of brides, folk medicine) would be restored to their rightful place. The social need for miraculous events was to be used as a means of exerting a socio-psychological influence on believers in the African context.

Vita Kimba is seen today as the first (female) Christian to create an independent African church which represented an absolutely new cultural and historical phenomenon. In this early Christian prophetic movement, ritual cults, customs and traditions, hierarchy, ceremonies, clothing and dances, use of the Old Testament as a basis, plastic representation of elements of the faith based on ghosts, reincarnated dead, animal sacrifices etc. all were not mere "exoticism" but rather to be explained in terms of the historical background and conditions.

Her supporters were no doubt deeply impressed by the fact that an "uneducated" woman was preaching in this way. Just as the traditional soothsayers and healers were supposed to be possessed by the ghosts of their ancestors, so, in this case, it was Saint Anthony who possessed Donna Béatrice and channelled his revelations through her. The African Christian church aimed to restore the old beliefs and customs and allow the old myths to return.

A catholic priest had Vita Kimba brought before the royal Congolese court, accused of treason and heresy, and condemned to death. She was burned at the stake on the 1st July 1706 with the name of Jesus on her lips. After her execution, the prophetic movement continued to exist under a successor, and Vita Kimba's teachings persisted in the Congo for a long time, despite all attempts to suppress them.

Orthodox Christianity developed in a unique way in Africa in the form of the Ethiopian-Coptic church. In Ethiopia, the oldest of the African kingdoms, Christianity took on traditional African elements and developed into a form which made of "the salvation of Man through adherence to the Law" a theological principle which was almost as important as salvation through faith and through the mystery of Christian mercy. "There are now in Abyssinia perhaps more churches than in any other part of the Christian world," stated the British traveller Harris in the middle of the 19th century, "and anyone building one believes that he has thereby absolved himself of sin ... Round in shape, with a door facing all four points of the compass, each little church has a brass cross on its conical straw roof ..., tambourines and crutches hang from the roof beams in a picturesque muddle." (40) Ethiopian churches varied from simple, almost impoverished prayer-houses in the provinces to rich, sumptuous buildings such as Trinity Cathedral in the

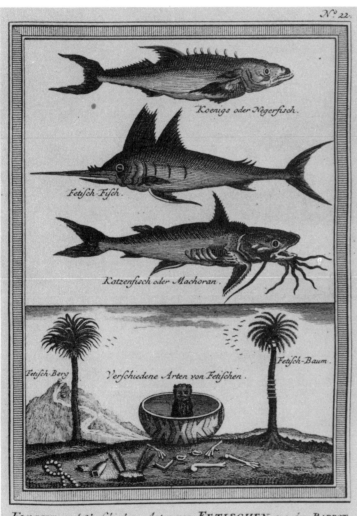

103

There were good and evil magic figures; the former could heal, the latter brought about the death or illness of an enemy. Fetishes. Book illustration. From: *General History of Voyages by Land and Sea...*, Leipzig 1747. Forschungsbibliothek Gotha.

capital; some were hidden in gigantic caves or perched on the tops of pinnacles which seemed barely climbable. Paul Jacob Bruns, in his description of 1793, wrote that in the Ethiopian church "in particular the Virgin Mary is worshipped to such an extent that to the Ethiopians the Catholic monks and missionaries who have lived among them appear to be despisers of Mary. In addition to the 31st of the month, there are a total of 32 annual feast days dedicated to the Mother of God, Queen of Heaven and Holiest of all Holies (for it is with these titles that she is honoured)." (26)

The Ethiopian-Coptic church provided the basis for an emancipatory movement which is derogatorily referred to in most literature of the time as the "cult of possession".

Based on the myth that "the Virgin Mary is the Creator of the World", emotional forms of belief and ceremonies were developed, above all in the old Christian provinces, in which the evil spirit Zar was central. Not only were vows made to this evil spirit, but also the blood of a sacrificial animal, mixed with fat and butter, was dedicated to it. In connection with this conservative tradition, which was in some cases linked with extreme sacrificial practices, there developed a "cult of possession" which occupied a dubious position between the New and the Old, but nevertheless it appears to have provided oppressed women with a new weapon.

"Among Ethiopian women", reported F. Heyer in his book *The Church of Ethiopia* (1971), "there is a strange form of possession called Zar. The night before important church festivals, above all at New Year, one can hear coming from one house a great tumult of women from the neighbourhood, clapping of hands and beating of drums. There are some villages in which up to a quarter of the women living there celebrate a night of possession once or twice a year ... These possessed women scream, speak as though in sleep, fall to the ground, cover their faces with the shamma, beat their heads on the ground or their bodies with a stick, they rush out and climb up a tree,

or eat burning coals. The Ethiopians are constantly astonished by the fact that the next day they display no traces whatsoever of their irrational behaviour."

Were these the effects of a type of "shamanism", the setting up of "links with the spiritual world" as, for example, occured among ancient North-American or Siberian peoples, who took narcotics in order to achieve a specific goal, usually ending up in a state of ecstasy? Was it a kind of epileptic fit induced by drugs, when, after such religious happenings, those taking part ended up with their bodies in a momentary state of unconsciousness, their limbs twitching, their muscles contracting? This is the only explanation for the fact that the women were able to prophesy exactly when they would be possessed by the Zar. The possibility that drugs, which were handed down from one generation of women to the next, were being used, cannot be dismissed at any rate. "Often this possession is inherited by an eldest daughter or daughter-in-law from her mother. The spirit's attacks occur when an individual is alone. Usually the women know when one is about to occur. They prepare themselves, weave special clothes which they keep for these occasions, adorn themselves with strings of pearls, which everyone knows are kept specifically for this purpose. They scatter fresh grass on the floor of their hut, and prepare coffee. Food prepared for the Zar cannot be touched by anyone else before it has been tasted by him. The Zar informs his victim whether a hen or a sheep has to be sacrificed, and further of what colour it should be."

Despite the ambiguity between progressive and conservative tendencies, between tradition and innovation, the "possession cult" of Ethiopian women should, in the last analysis, be seen as a dangerous and harmful aspect of religions and cults, especially in view of the role played by drugs.

Women defended their rights most successfully within polytheistic religions in which they served as priestesses or as members of communities of priestesses, which often amounted to secret societies for women. It should be said immediately that there were, in Africa, more men's societies than women's ones, and the latter, despite their relatively large numbers, were the exception rather than the rule. The reasons for this can be found in the early history of the secret societies, which came into being in the transitional period after the break-up of the original gentile society and took the form of, usually, supra-regional societal and religious associations whose members often secured economic and social advantages for themselves. The male societies claimed power over women and young people, and adhered to patrilinear norms. They held secret meetings, were sworn to silence vis-à-vis non-members, sat in judgement and punished wrong-doers. These societies often competed with the power of the chief. When they appeared in public, masks played an important role, as, for example, described in some detail by the French ethnographer M. Griaule, in his book *Masques Dogons*, Paris 1938. Masked rituals, masked dances, religious songs and communal sacrifices were all important parts of their activities. The societies were seen as mediators between the living and the dead, preservers of tradition, and they also had an oracular and healing function. As Griaule reported, only a few selected women were permitted to attend the celebrations—"sisters of the masks"—to produce the ritual millet-beer which the men drank in large quantities. (81)

Even though these societies were predominantly male, female equivalents did exist—in Sierra Leone, Mali, Upper Volta, the Ivory Coast, and among the inhabitants of the jungles and savannas of West and Central Africa and north and south of the Rovuma across to the east coast of Africa. These female secret societies preferred sculptures to masks—usually of female figures, often representations of a mother and child.

H. C. Monrad describes some interesting details in his account of a journey to West Africa, which seem to suggest that the members of these female societies were able to defend themselves with some success

104

Women were instrumental in preserving traditions. Among the settled rural peasants the cult of ancestors was important in this respect. Ancestral figure. Bayanzi, Zaïre. Museum für Völkerkunde, Hamburg.

against the exaggerated claims of the men to privilege and power. "If a man marries one of these women, he has to recognize her authority ..." If the man failed to adhere to the rules of equal co-existence, she had certain means at her disposal with which to pursue her rights. "If such a woman feels wronged by her husband, she behaves as though she were mad, smears her body with white earth, clay or mud, ties grass and reeds round her head and other parts of her body, and walks or crawls, at least when she is being observed, from one village to another ... When she goes out on to the streets she is usually armed with a club in each hand. The negroes cluster around her and watch her gesticulating, singing and dancing. Sometimes she hits the spectators on the head or any other part of their bodies she can reach with her clubs. This behaviour is maintained until her husband or whoever she is angry at appeases her by making sacrifices to the fetish, giving the usual presents, most of which are taken by her and her sisters. The whole farce ends with gay dancing to the honour of the fetish." The author goes on to say of the regular meetings of these women's societies and the close relationship between the women: "These women often gather in the villages in order, as they put it, to dance fetish, i.e. to amuse themselves with dances in honour of the fetish. They smear their entire bodies with red earth, but their faces with white earth, attire themselves so scantily that not even those parts of their bodies which modesty forbids mentioning are covered, and dance round in a circle with the most lewd gestures and movements, one after the other, without holding hands. Their music is provided by the senior fetish-women, who stand in the centre of the circle and sing in harsh voices ... At a meeting of several thousand women in 1807 it is said that an epidemic illness broke out which eliminated most of them." (36)

One cannot help seeing certain parallels between Africa and Europe. In the Middle Ages in Europe the important role played by women in social religious movements seems also to have been motivated not so

105

For centuries, women were at the centre of many holy places, magical activities and oracular events. Hunting magic. Woman invokes a female deer. Rock drawing.

much by a greater religious faith compared with men, but rather by a desire for emancipation. In some cases, in the African context, even where on first glance no activities of women's societies are immediately identifiable, they were nevertheless active. The following extracts from voyagers' accounts bear witness to this.

It was reported of the inhabitants of Dahomey that a "brotherhood of women" used to guard the holy places. Here, too, processions took place in which only girls and women participated. John Duncan wrote about one of the "fetish-women": "Her clothes were of the strangest sort. She wore a very large headdress made of grass or reeds in the form of a turned-up hat, and round her neck were several magic amulets. Her robes consisted of a thick skirt made of grass stalks which were attached at one end to a band about four feet long. This is put round the body so that the unattached ends of the grass hang down rather like a kilt, only affording less covering than the latter. On such festive occasions the fetish-woman also wears a sheep's or a goat's skull on her head and in each hand a thick stick made of wood. She dances to the music she produces by hitting these sticks together, moving with as much grace as a load of hay which a mower pitches with his fork. Her body is painted with a very fine white paste prepared from oyster shells." (42)

In 1833, Richard and John Lander reported on women's societies among the Hausa in their book *Voyage in Africa to explore the Niger to its estuary*: "Today a colourful procession of women devoted to the old religion went through the town, sometimes walking, sometimes dancing, and holding in their hands large, shady branches. When we saw her, the priestess had just drunk fetish-water, and was being carried on the shoulders of one of the pious women, who was aided by two others who supported the trembling arms and hands of their mistress..." The number of women in this procession was, however, fairly limited. "The total number of women forming this singular procession must have been between 90 and 100. All of them were

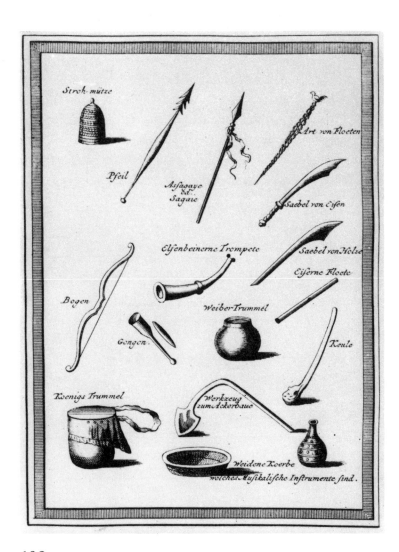

106

Craftsmen produced many objects mainly for use by women. Weapons and musical instruments from the Widah kingdom. From: *General History of Voyages by Land and Sea...*, Leipzig 1747. Forschungsbibliothek Gotha.

Women and Religious Cults

in their best apparel and their movements were accompanied from time to time by drums and pipes and their wild voices with which they joined in the music. Now they divided into pairs and, with the branches, which they swung over their heads, they formed one of the most extraordinary and grotesque spectacles which the human mind can imagine ..." The authors did not fail to bring the female representatives of traditional beliefs into disrepute, as is betrayed by the language alone. "Towards midday the female worshippers of the old gods, of whom we have already spoken, celebrated a second, secret ceremony, as laid down by their religion, and then, as in the previous case, processed through the streets. When all was over, and the procession had finally broken up, several of them, accompanied by musicians with flutes, drums, guitars and many small boys and girls, paid me a visit without revealing their intentions ... The priestess herself (was) fantastically dressed up as a man ..." This male apparel crops up in countless other examples in which emancipatory women always attempted to look outwardly like men. Richard and John Lander stressed the role of the princesses in the religious ceremonies. "The religion to which these zealots adhere and which until recently predominated in the country, is still held in great respect, to such an extent that the daughters of the king are at an early age initiated into its secrets. Without exception they take part in all the superstitious customs and ceremonies, and one of them is even a priestess." (39) The role played by African women in religious cults is an example of the complex and contradictory role played by religious ideology vis-à-vis progressive movements. In Islam and Christianity such movements anyhow only had a place as oppositional movements in those times. However, the examples of tribal and polytheistic religions show that the remains of matrilinearity found a home in them.

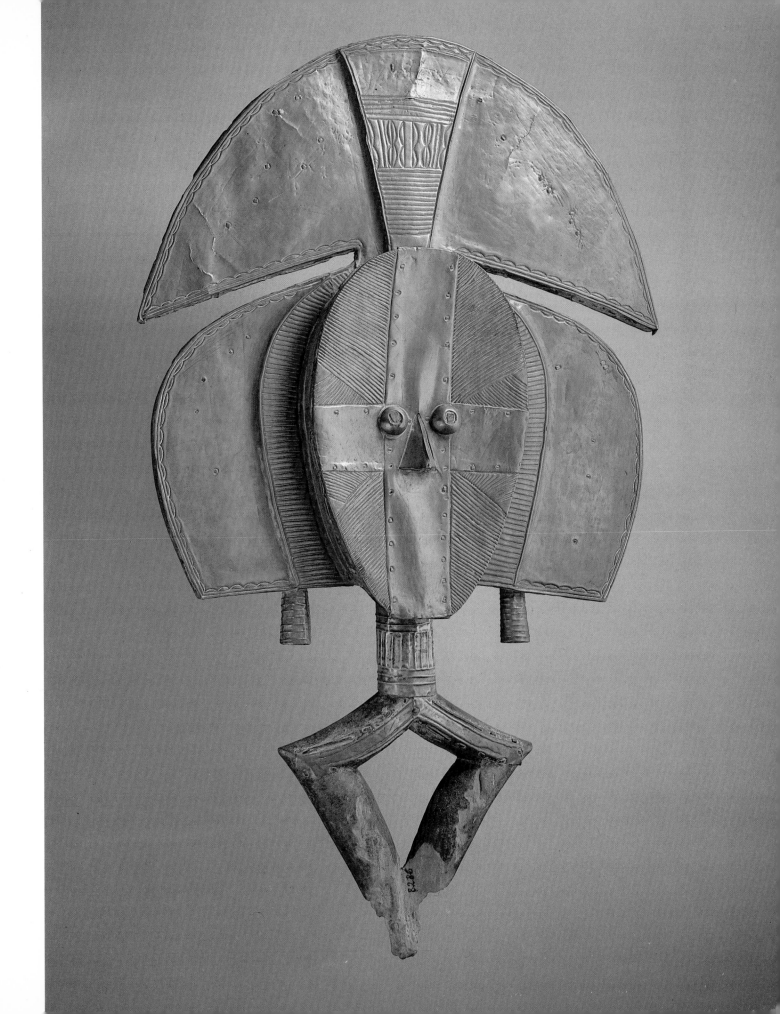

107

The belief in an "Original Mother" is found in many parts of Africa. Human beings were only one of the manifestations of life in nature, and death meant merely a change in the form of one's existence. Mother goddess or death spirit. Bakuba. Völkerkundemuseum of the University of Zurich.

108

The traditional worship of ancestors did not allow a rapid transition from matrilinear to patrilinear systems. For a long time elements of matrilinearity remained. Depiction of an ancestor. Female half-figure. Height 26 cm. Wood. Southeastern Zaïre. Staatliches Museum für Völkerkunde, Linden-Museum, Stuttgart.

109

Sculptures of ancestors, the "Original Mother" or also mythical animals displayed a high degree of artistic sophistication. Ancestor figure. Rautenstrauch-Joest-Museum, Cologne.

110

In West Africa the "Original Mother" is depicted as a figure with a large bust sitting on a seat. During the initiation ceremony participants in the nighttime procession beat the ground rhythmically in order to request the deity to grant a good harvest and many offspring. Depiction of ancestor. Seated female figure. Height 30 cm. Senufo. Staatliches Museum für Völkerkunde, Linden-Museum, Stuttgart.

Mask of mother. Among
the Dan-Ngere tribes the
religious secret society
used the "Dan" mask
which represented the
ideal of a beautiful
woman. She was the
"mother of masks" and
exercised various func-
tions in the village and in
the initiation camp: she
conciliated in quarrels,
cared for infants, warded
off witches, taught myths,
singing rhythm and rhe-
toric. West Africa. Völ-
kerkundemuseum of the
University of Zurich.

112

In the border areas of
Liberia, Sierra Leone and
Guinea the Mende tribe
used carved wooden fig-
ures in their soothsaying
ceremonies which de-
picted a standing woman
with slim hands and
feet. Figure of a woman.
Mende, West Africa.
Rautenstrauch-Joest-
Museum, Cologne.

113

The Bambara carved fig-
ures with characteristic
sharp geometrical facial
features. These depicted
the "Original Mother",
fertility of women and of
the land. Female figure.
Wood. 40 × 9.5 cm.
Bambara, West Sudan.
Rautenstrauch-Joest-
Museum, Cologne.

114

Being guardians of tradi-
tion proved a protection
for women against in-
equality and reduction in
social status. Stylized figure of female ancestor.
Wood. Rautenstrauch-
Joest-Museum, Cologne.

115

The "Original Mother" was worthy of supporting the seat of the tribal chief. Such carved stools were the prerogative of the rulers alone. Ritual objects, names, rocks and trees carried symbolic meaning. Stool of a chief. Museum für Völkerkunde, Hamburg.

116

Even today the influence of religion can be felt— the environment and all actions and events are seen from a religious point of view and understood and interpreted accordingly. Magic figures were modelled on anthropomorphic spirits of nature which, it was believed, gave life to one's surroundings and were to be feared. Large anthropomorphic figure. Height 155 cm. Cameroon. Staatliches Museum für Völkerkunde, Linden-Museum, Stuttgart.

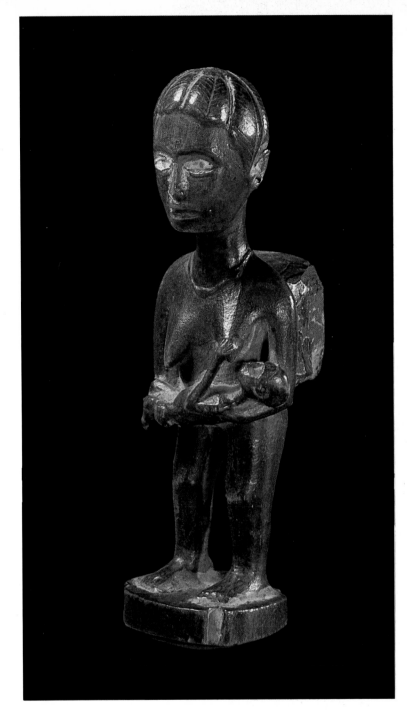

117

Female figure from the Bakongo. Cylindrical containers sealed with glass which held magic objects and substances, so-called magic figures, were common in many parts of the Lower Congo region. Museum für Völkerkunde, Frankfurt/Main.

118

Magic figure. Wood, decorated with human teeth. Height 38 cm. Ba Songye, Batampa, Zaïre. Museum für Völkerkunde, Frankfurt/Main.

119

Wooden mask with bast
fringe depicting an old
woman. A requisite of
the Bundu women's
society, around 1930.
Height 40 cm. Liberia.
Museum für Völker-
kunde, Dresden.

This store-room door
from Dogon bears rows
of male and female
figures. They represent
ancestors or protective
spirits. Museum für
Völkerkunde, Leipzig.

121

During the initiation ceremony, masks were worn by girls in long simple dresses made of woven straw which completely covered the dancers. "Zoba" mask of the female secret society "Sande". Height 50 cm. Black stained wood. Vai, Liberia. Historisches Museum, Bern.

122

Women enjoyed a position of respect. Among freestanding sculptured figures in most areas of Africa female ones predominated. Female figure. Museum für Völkerkunde, Vienna.

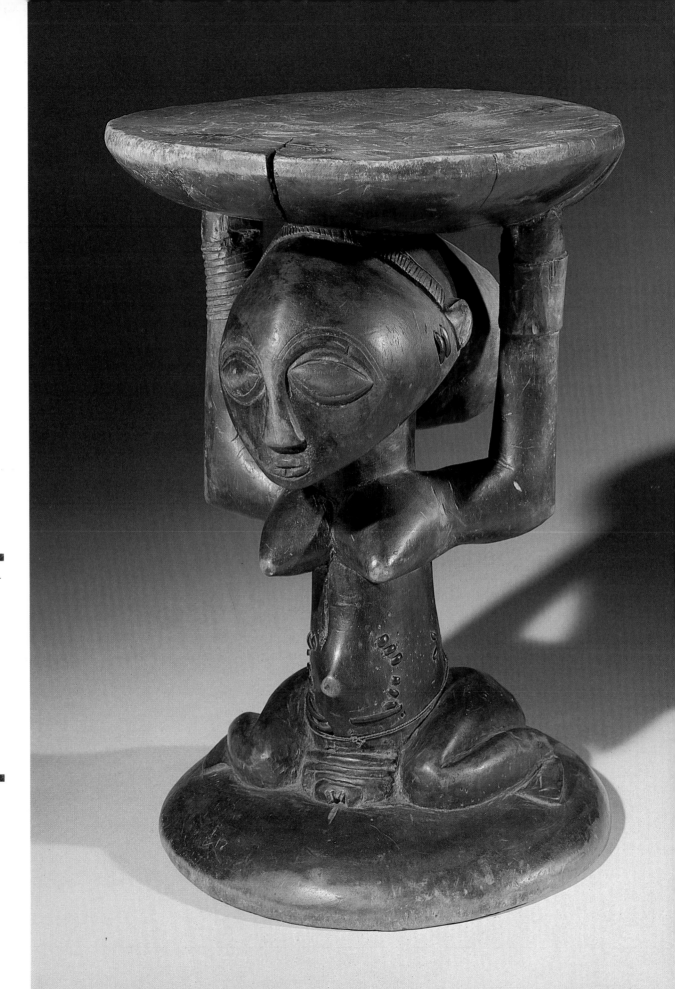

123

Kabila or Mboko figure.
Wood. Height 29 cm.
Luba, Southeastern
Zaïre. Staatliches Mu-
seum für Völkerkunde,
Linden-Museum,
Stuttgart.

124

Masks of the Ibo, a tribe
on the Niger. Museum
für Völkerkunde, Leipzig.

125

Weaving. Wall hanging.
Museum für Völker-
kunde, Vienna.

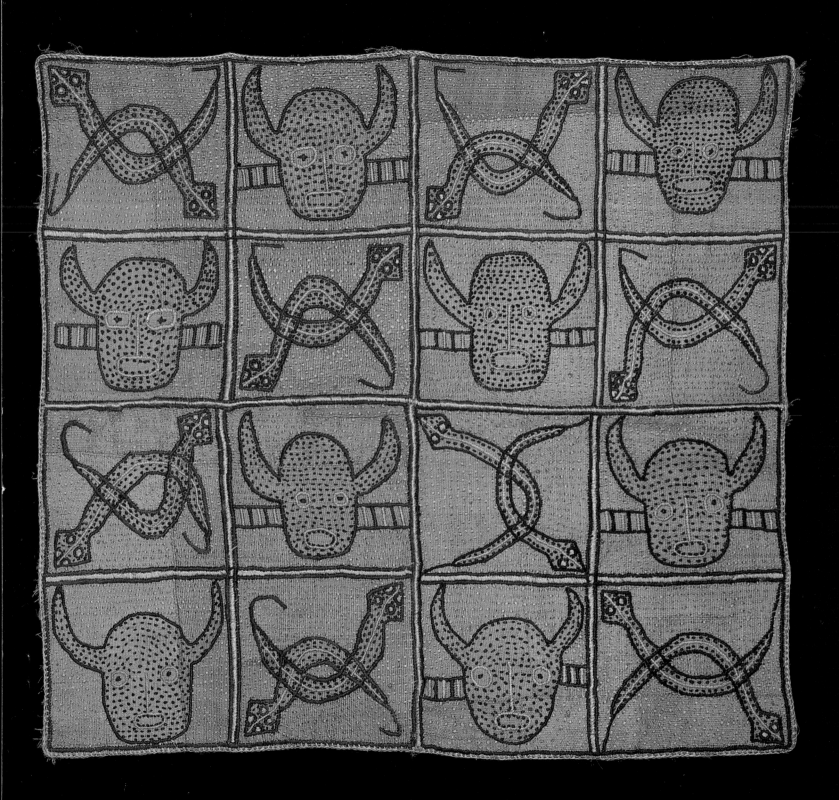

AFRICAN WOMEN AND ART

Folk-art in Africa did not pass on the names of its creators to the next generation. If we are to speak of the role of women in the art of old Africa then what we are concerned with foremost is establishing which areas women were able to express their creativity in: in ceramics and textiles, decorative wall-painting, music and poetry. One or two forms of expression—e.g. decorative ornamentation—have already been mentioned.

Only two areas are known in which women were on an equal footing as men as sculptors. In the Congo, women of the Mangbetu produced famous pots decorated with sculptured heads with high hairstyles, and in Cameroon ceramic dishes with human and animal motifs were created. Women, however, had a virtual monopoly of ordinary domestic pottery, and they also had some influence as assistants to woodcarvers. The extraordinary feel which women had for the beautifully decorated dishes and pots which they produced is constantly praised by art historians. From an art-historical point of view the most interesting objects are pots made of wood and clay and also decorated calabashes. Wooden vessels and ceramics often imitated the forms of humans and animals.

Among the Bakuba in the Congo the so-called "bongotos"—richly ornamented boards or imitations of everyday objects or animals made of redwood—formed an important element in their artistic production. Women mixed a powder out of palm-oil and sand, formed and decorated the tiny works of art and heated them over the fire. These "bongotos" also served as a popular method of payment.

Women were also responsible for decoration of the living quarters, the production of kitchen utensils and of children's toys, such as dolls. Particularly well-known are the decorative paintings found on the walls of the houses. While among the Yoruba the men were excellent woodcarvers and carved the wooden posts and the doors of their homes, the women also decorated their houses both inside and out. Their wall-paintings displayed both a high level of artistic skill and excellent powers of observation. In the wall-paintings of West Africa (Guinea, Liberia, Nigeria, and other countries) scenic representations predominated. Traditional themes—the power and wealth of the chiefs, battle victories and hunting exploits, or ritual dances with costumes and masks—were gradually complemented by scenes from everyday life. The colours used were white (kaolin), yellow (ocre), reddish brown (laterite), and black (peat), often in up to fifteen shades, including greenish and reddish tones. Before use, the earth was made into mud and its durability increased by the addition of plant glue. In East Africa, where wall-painting was not so widespread, it tended to take the form of simple geometric patterns. In South Africa the Matabele were famous for their wall-paintings. Ornamented stucco, for example in Mauritania, was also said to be the work of women, who were also responsible for renewing or repairing it after the annual rainy season. We have already mentioned the production of richly decorated cloth made of various types of material, under the headings "Craft-work artivities" and "Work and formal dress, jewellery, body care".

As poets, women used to create love songs and work songs. Music and dance were further areas where they expressed their creativity. However, it was rare that women danced alone or in groups. At most dances, it was the men, in full costume, who led, and the women usually only made music and kept the beat. However, there were female dances which took place in connection with religious and other celebrations, and a type of female dancer did develop, for example in the temples. The French Abbé Proyart gives an eyewitness account: "Women have their meetings, just like men, at which they dance and disport themselves, but only on feast days or when they have finished work in the fields or in the home. They never interfere in the male gatherings; a wife does not dance with her husband nor a sister with her brother." (19)

Often these female dances joined with the male ones. Thus L. Wolf, in 1885, describes a dance of the Lukengo among the Bakuba. The men's dances alternated with those of the women and girls, whose steps and movements were different from those of the men and consisted of shifting from one leg to the other, displaying an extraordinary agility of their hips, and turning in all directions, with their left hand, fingers spread, high above their head and their right hand pointing straight downwards. The movements of their fingers and wrists always followed those of their hips. Rhythm was provided by clapping of hands and beating of drums, but the women were also capable of playing other instruments.

But women were not just artists themselves, but also popular subjects for artistic activities. Since the very earliest times, when hunters and gatherers in Africa started to create drawings and sculptures on rocks or on the walls of the caves in which they sheltered from the sun and rain, portraits of women have played an important role.

Examples of this can be found in the area at present covered by the Sahara. This and neighbouring regions looked entirely different about three thousand years and more B.C. In the mountains there grew cypresses, pines, juniper and acacia trees. Rivers thousands of kilometres in length flowed across the land. Beside countless lakes lived elephants, rhinoceroses, lions, giraffes. The climate was Mediterranean in character. Archaeological excavations have produced sufficient evidence of the "paradisical" past which the Sahara had—one in which there was ample opportunity for raising animals, hunting, and cultivating the land. In the Neolithic Age cultivation was finally established in addition to animal husbandry. Between 3000 and 2000 B.C., the geological process of drying-out of the Sahara occurred, caused by climatic changes which marked the end of the damp Neolithic period. Gradually there developed a desert area largely devoid of human life, apart from some nomadic animal-rearers.

The fact that this region once had a blossoming civilization can be seen from the impressive rock and cave drawings which were found along the old trade-routes linking the interior of Africa to the Mediterranean coast. These pictures of people and animals, warriors with chariots, women and men, grouped into scenes, give us an idea of what life was like in those times. Archaeologists have investigated the majority of these works of art which have survived from one of the earliest periods of human history. The most important rock and cave drawings to be found outside the Sahara were discovered in East and South Africa. The French scientist Henri Lhote investigated more than 10,000 rock drawings in the Sahara, including the "White Lady" or horned goddess, which was discovered in Auanrhet. "From the wet surface of the stone there emerged the graceful silhouette of a woman, striding towards some goal. One leg was slightly bent, and the other stretched backwards over the ground. At her knees, her belt and her outstretched arms there were fine fringes. On either side of her head, above the horizontal horns, was a broad stippled area like a cloud of grains over a field of corn ... The woman's body was coloured pale yellowish bordered with white, and her shoulders, stomach and lower back were covered with strange decorative motifs: white dotted parallel lines with occasional red strokes." (103) Also discovered were representations of a hut, men with axes in their hands, women in front of cooking pots, and other everyday scenes. Among the life-sized pictures (which are ascribed to the Neolithic period between 5000 and 1200 B.C.) one of the most significant is the one of a "seated man and seated woman". Another one worthy of particular mention is the superb female figure "Antinea" (*c.* 1200 B.C.)

The position of women in African art and culture is important for two reasons. Firstly it supplements our picture of women in Africa from the earliest times and adds new, interesting aspects; and secondly this part of material and spiritual civilization represents a basic source of information for archaeologists, ethnographers, linguists, theologians and, not least, historians. To this extent, therefore, statements about the place of women in African art are also statements about women in general.

In this context, archaeological finds are worthy of mention first. Again and again the Ife and Benin cultures crop up in this connection, and also—an important early source—the Nok culture, which made it possible in the first place to classify positively the Ife and Benin bronzes as products of old African tradition and culture.

In the 1940s the English archaeologist Bernard Fagg discovered in Central Africa, not far from the settlement of Nok, large numbers of terracotta statues, including ones of women, animals, stone and metal tools, and other objects. As mentioned already on page 22, this hitherto unknown culture was named the Nok culture, and dated as being between 500 B.C. and 200 A.D. The finds are thus the oldest known sculptures in West Africa. Despite the lack of direct analogies, they display important features which were typical for later traditional sculpture.

In the early 20th century the well-known German archaeologist and ethnographer, Leo Frobenius, discovered, in the southwestern part of what is today Nigeria, the Ife sculptures, which shattered the previously-held opinion in Europe that African sculpture was not anything more than the art of "primitive peoples" capable only of creating wooden carvings. The many terracotta sculptures he found included some female figures.

In 1938, in the same area, on the site of an old palace, 20 bronze sculptures were discovered. It is assumed that these decorated the holy altar of someone's ancestors, but it is not clear whom the male and female heads were supposed to represent. Only one bust was identified as being one of the ancient rulers. Further finds in 1949 and 1953 of terracotta sculptures in the holy groves of Abiri and Iwinria, and also the discovery, in 1957, of a complete bronze figure, further extended knowledge of the stylistic variety of the Ife sculptures, and showed that they represent a special form of traditional Nigerian sculpture. Scientists postulate that the school of sculpture reached its peak in the period of the 12th–14th centuries.

Among the sculptures, in addition to the idealized representation of a warrior hero and the dynamic face of a ruler who was worshipped as a god, one finds the poetic face of a young girl and the arrogant face of a female ruler. The mature style of these works, and their high degree of technical sophistication bear witness to a long process of artistic and technical development. The Ife sculpture reflects the social and aesthetic ideals which were characteristic of the work of the "courtly" school of artists. The basic lines of this ancient art can still be found in the art of the Yoruba tribes in Nigeria. This strong link can also be seen in the details of the ornaments, the highly decorative jewellery, large beads and necklaces, which were worn from time immemorial. This is seen also in the tribal tattoos which are found not just in the woodcarvings of the Yoruba and Ibo in Nigeria, but also on the bodies of the inhabitants of the modern state of Zaïre.

Closely connected with the Ife artefacts were those of Benin, famous throughout the world, and dating probably from a period between the 15th century and the first half of the 17th century. Most of the surviving objects are made of bronze or ivory. The famous bronze heads of the queen mother (of which more than ten survive) date from the earlier part of the period (early 16th century). Often they are life-sized heads, produced to preserve the memory of dead kings and queen mothers, which were originally placed on altars. The "bronze belt" stretched along the Niger. Along the entire west bank miniature sculpture was produced in moulds—for example the famous weights used for weighing out gold-dust. These were found among the Ashanti in Ghana, along the Gold Coast and in Dahomey. The discovery of the sculptures in all these areas contradicted the general opinion of the Europeans that the negro cultures could only produce wooden ones. Among the many terracotta, ceramic and bronze sculptures, heads of men and women were found in equal numbers. In addition to terracotta heads, whole decorated figures were found, arm and foot bangles, and mother-of-pearl jewellery etc.

From the very earliest African cultures onwards, figures of mother and child played an important role, often with the sexual characteristics much exaggerated. No erotic effect was intended, but rather the artists wished merely to underline the differences; and often female characteristics were linked with fertility magic in myths and religions.

The ravages of termites and of the climate have meant that most of the wooden sculptures which have survived are not more than about 200 years old. But they clearly bear witness to a much older artistic tradition. This can be seen, too, in their content, the way in which the representation of woman successfully combines all parts of the sculpture in order to make maximum impact on the observer: the feeling of heaviness or weightlessness, solemnity or grace. Among the Congo sculptures there are many which consist of one or two symmetrically posed female figures. They sit, with bended legs, on their heels, and carry on their outstretched hands or on their heads a large flat bowl. Some sources say these were seats, others identify

126

Much loving care was devoted to the creation of jewellery. In West Africa bracelets, bangles and rings were produced using a melted wax technique. Leg bangles. Museum für Völkerkunde, Hamburg.

them as tables for the throwing of oracular grains. Of particular interest are the elaborate hairstyles, which often are as bulky as the heads themselves. The hair hangs symmetrically to both sides of the rounded rump, which is foreshortened and attached to the folded thighs.

The African sculptors concentrated on expressing only the essential features in their representations of women. Even though the basic features remained standard over centuries, the faces of the wooden sculptures, even if they were not based directly on a model, were developed with countless variants. Particular attention was paid to the nose, eyes and mouth. Thus there were "antique" eyes—almond-shaped, slightly curved eyes without pupils, sometimes framed with narrow lids. There were also similarly shaped eyes but with a thin slit cutting them lengthways. Round holes represented seeing eyes.

The artists displayed great powers of observation and attention to detail in their sketching of various scenes involving female figures: sometimes a woman carrying a child on her back, a meal round a fire, and other compositions involving multiple figures.

Even if nothing is known of the personalities of the black sculptors and little about their working conditions and social status, then at least the portraits of women which they created tell us something about the ideals which they had, and the enthusiasm which they felt. Beauty was for them linked with goodness. In the language of the Wolof in Senegal, goodness was a word which young men used to refer to a beautiful young girl. Beauty was for them a "promise of happiness". Thus a young girl who wore a wooden mask was greeted with the following words:

There is a head, a beautiful head
All men look
All women look
All children look
All dogs look ....

Myths, fairy tales, sagas and proverbs also help to complete our picture of some of the characteristics of women in the Africa of bygone days.

Often a reference to love is found in proverbs. Thus one reads: "For the sickness of love there is no doctor." The Chagga in East Africa say maliciously: "There is no woman who says to another: wash your face". The Swaheli, even more rudely, say: "A woman is clothes". "The soul of a mother is full of sympathy"—praises motherly love. In Togo they say: "When a child is hungry, that shows that its mother is also." The Herero have an even stronger saying: "Let your father die, but do not let your mother".

Verses from a love song of the Hausa show their rich poetic diction even in translation:

Mabruka, daughter of our country,
With eyes gleaming like stars!
...

Mabruka, my flesh and blood
My heart, I am good to you!
My heart is fallen sick
On account of Mabruka
...

Mabruka is a camel girl
With her slender neck.
Her teeth are like gold,
Her arms are slender as sticks.
Her nose is like a rose,
Her face is like a mirror,
Her feet are red with henna.
Her shoes are of gold,
Her headcloth is of gold,
Like gold is her hair,
Her loin-cloth is embroidered with silver,
Her blouse is all embroidered with silver,
Her trousers are of silk,
Her breasts are like a silver vessel—
Look at her bosom,

It dazzles yours eyes!
Look at her figure,
It sways like a reed!

In a dancing song of the Swaheli, a partner's fidelity is the theme. The song, much shortened in translation, runs:

Give me the seat and I shall sit down
To Mananazi I sing in my slumbers,
I sing my song to my wife,
And forget all pain and cares.
At the door she always waits
As soon as I go down the steps
To do my business in town.
At once she calls to the servants:
"O Sada and Rehema, hurry!"
Says she, "and take good care,
Cook quickly and do not tarry,
Cook rice and tasty sauce."
And if I stay too long she sends
A servant "O find him, where is he?
Ah, he has gone to the palace,
Or no, perhaps to a minister.

Perhaps he is seeing friends,
O go and seek him out
At his brother's, his mother's, his aunt's,
What are you waiting for?

And then tell him how I am waiting,
Say: Master your true love is calling!
Tell him I am tired and waiting,
I am standing waiting and crying.

And let him pass politely,
Ah, he should bring me new joys
When he comes—and follow him prettily
With his scent of musk and amber."

And then he enters and greets her,
Heja's child hurries towards him,
She hurries to lay her sweet hands
On her husband's shoulders.

And he speaks, turned to the highest:
"That you may grant her prayer!"
And thus have I finished this song
In honour of my treasure, Mananazi.

Women also appeared in sagas and fairy tales. The following shortened story of the beautiful Tjaratjondjorondjondjo comes from the repertoire of the Herero:

"There was once a woman who had a very beautiful daughter. Nobody ever tired of looking at her. And she was well looked after. The village was large and contained many girls, some of them beautiful. And they were most joyous. They would look after the lambs as they grazed. But all those who saw the girl asked: Who does that beautiful child belong to? And the other girls told them. Then the people felt desire when they went past and always wanted to marry them all. One day, all the girls gathered together. Among them was the girl whose name was Tjaratjondjorondjondjo. And they went to the shepherds and said to them: Now, boys, we are of course all beautiful, but which of us is the most beautiful? And they replied: Of course you are all beautiful, but Tjaratjondjorondjondjo is twice as beautiful as Mbazuva and Rutangarauane. And Tjaratjondjorondjondjo rejoiced. And they asked all the berry-pickers, but they said the same as all the young men. And the girls gestured to each other and said: Let them, tomorrow is another day. The next day all the girls agreed to do away with Tjaratjondjorondjondjo. They put their plan into operation, and the girl's beauty became her downfall."

It was not just with love songs that African women took part in poetic literature. On many points we remain in the dark because authorship could only be established with certainty after the emergence of writing and the introduction of the Arabic and Latin alphabets (with the exception of Ethiopia). The first known poetess of African origin was a girl from Senegal, who was taken as a 7-year-old slave to America in 1761 and was named Phillis Wheatley after her Boston owner. She was something of a "child prodigy". Several of her poems were published, the first when she was only seventeen. Her collected works were reprinted several times. (94)

Researchers and missionaries, voyagers of discovery, and artists, all brought back information from the old African kingdoms century after century. The perception of these Europeans of life on the Dark Continent was, of course, coloured by their own culture. Their impressions of Africa were very much in line with the prevailing view in Europe of African conditions. Negative reports coexisted with objective opinions, pictures and descriptions. One important source which had an influence on the Europeans' view of Africa were the various travellers' accounts. These often made mention of the remarkable form and beauty of women in Africa. Thus, in a voyager's account of the hinterland of Senegal one can read: "The female sex is of superior beauty to those at the estuary of the Senegal, although the latter generally have prettily-shaped faces. They are well-formed, well-educated, have proud but smouldering eyes, and soft voices. They are much more amorous than the Jalof (Wolof); their clothes, too, are more original and more stylish. Their hair is curled like that of European ladies. Their heads are covered by caps from which glass beads, pieces of amber and coral hang down. On their necks, ears and arms are golden rings and bangles. Their clothing is scanty... Their singing is tasteful and pleasing, their songs soulful, their music less noisy than that of the Jalof (Wolof) and the instruments more tasteful and artistic in themselves." (33)

Brodie Cruickshank in *Eighteen years on the African Gold Coast* (1855) describes the beauty of the Africans in the following words: "There is, in young African girls a pleasing liveliness and gaiety, and a softness which imbues all their movements with beauty and charm ... In their every look, their every spontaneous, graceful movement, one reads youth, health, lightness and agility."

The women's charm and liveliness are praised repeatedly: "Is not beauty made up of the greatest clean-

127

Based on a traveller's report from the year 1505, Hans Burgkmair created a series of six woodcuts, the *African Picturebook*. Family scene.

liness, glowing health, charming modesty, combined with a restrained desire to please, great beauty of the figure, often with a pretty, oval face, sparkling eyes, perfect teeth, and an excellent skin which, just as with whites, changes colour according to their emotions." (43)

Book illustrations deserve a special mention. Impressive pictures of African women were to be found in the voyagers' accounts, usually penned by Italians, Portuguese, Dutchmen, Frenchmen, Englishmen and Germans. Thus, in the book by the Portuguese O. López *A True and Actual Description of the Kingdom of Congo in Africa* (6), many women and scenes are illustrated, which may more often than not, on the surface, be modelled more on European women than on African ones, but which express well the humanistic counter-current to colonial expansion and the early slave-trade.

The pictures of the copper engraver and publisher, Theodor de Bry (1528–98) and his sons date from this period—they were published between 1590 and 1634 in 25 volumes. It was not until later that emphasis was put on greater accuracy of detail. Thus Zacharias Wagner, at the beginning of the 17th century, painted a negress slave on the Nassau property in Brasil, who was branded with the mark of Count Moritz of Nassau; he portrayed her in a statuesque pose with her child, exact in every detail, right down to the clay pipe carried on her belt. This posed pair, who represented neither the everyday life nor the actual conditions of the average slave, was typical of the contemporary perception of the period of overseas slave-trade.

In increasing numbers, painters and sketchers accompanied the mid-19th century expeditions or prominent individuals who went on African safaris. Pictures of African women decorated travel books and in this way began to influence the thinking and the emotions of contemporaries. Before long, the dominant image was that of a woman with a basket on her head, a child on her back, a hoe in her hand, working in a field of maize.

African women can also be found in European Fine Art of the period. While representations of Africans were rare during the Romanesque and Gothic periods, from the 15th century onwards, and above all during the Renaissance, the inhabitants of the Dark Continent became increasingly a source of interest.

The drawing by Albrecht Dürer (1471–1528), created in 1521, of *Katherina, aged 20 years* is famous. What seems to interest the artist is not so much the anthropological features, as the desire to portray a "mooress" with individual features, in all her vigour and dignity. This representation is entirely comparable to the affectionate treatment found in the well-known portrait of Dürer's mother.

Hieronymus Bosch (1450–1516), in several parts of his picture *Garden of Delights* portrayed African men and women together with Europeans. In an open landscape "naked people peacefully united … members of various races, white and ebony-black, are portrayed in all their beauty and innocence."

Rosemarie Schuder, a German writer, writes of the picture's creator: "Surrounded by war, by murder, burning, rape and pillage, the terror of foreign despotism, the servile rejoicing of some of his fellow-countrymen, the general pettiness which prevailed at the time, he dreamt a dream of all-embracing justice which would come to all beings, Man or Woman, including even the blacks—the heathens. The *Garden of Delights* is a dream. Hieronymus Bosch is creating a counterpart to the reality of his times. He is dreaming of a peaceful, untroubled world."

In the series of woodcuts entitled *African Picturebook*, by Hans Burgkmair (1473–1531) which was created after the appearance of Balthasar Springer's travel report in 1505, we find, in one family scene, a superb, confident portrait of a Nama woman.

The Portuguese conquests of the early 16th century and the development of the slave-trade both led to a number of representations of Africans of both sexes in the role of servants. The Dutch artist Cornelis Cornelisz van Haerlem (1562–1638) portrays a black female

128

Many masks indicate the role and function of women as priests and soothsayers, as well as singers and poetesses. Female mask from the region of the Ogowe river. Völkerkundemuseum of the University of Zurich.

129

Over the centuries, each of the various peoples developed their own distinctive style and symbols. Clay vessel. Azande. Tropical Museum, Amsterdam.

130

Seated female figure.
Museum für Völker-
kunde, Hamburg.

131

Doll. Museum für
Völkerkunde, Hamburg.

132

The masks of the "Ge-lede" secret society of the Yoruba, West Africa, are painted yellowish, brown, violet and green. The upper part is decorated with the figure of a woman or a fabulous animal. Gelede mask from Addo, kingdom of Ketu. Height 16.5 cm, length 30 cm. Wood, repaired with tin. Historisches Museum, Bern.

133

Female mask. Rauten-strauch-Joest-Museum, Cologne.

134

Even in objects destined for a specific use, artistic considerations played an important role. Drinking vessel with ornament. Völkerkundemuseum of the University of Zurich.

135

Woven cloth, baskets and
plates were ornamented
almost everywhere. This
basket with lid of the
Danskil is decorated with
glass beads. Museum für
Völkerkunde, Leipzig.

136

Since the earliest times
when hunters and gather-
ers started to create pictures on rocks and in the
caves in which they shel-
tered from sun and rain,
right through the era of
kingdoms and down to
the present day, depic-
tions of women were
the commonest motifs.
Female figure, richly
decorated with jewellery.
Rautenstrauch-Joest-
Museum, Cologne.

137

A chief's stool, depicting
a female. Baluba, Zaïre.
Rautenstrauch-Joest-
Museum, Cologne.

138

Swaheli jewellery. Silver.
Museum für Völker-
kunde, Leipzig.

139

Ceremonial fans. Black
stained wood. Leather
strap. Length 25 cm,
breadth 14 cm. Histo-
risches Museum, Bern.

140

Hand-held mask from the Budu women's society. Mende, West Africa. Museum für Völkerkunde, Hamburg.

141

Discs such as these are parts of masks. Grasslands of Cameroon. Diameter 64 cm. Museum für Völkerkunde, Leipzig.

142

Depictions of the madonna were an important motif for early Ethiopian artists. Ethiopian art occupies a special position in Africa as a whole. Under the influence of the Coptic church there is an almost complete lack of three-dimensional depictions of human beings. Instead there are pictures with a religious content. Madonna with child, viewed from the side. Church of Abba Liguanos at Aksum. Institut für Denkmalpflege, Berlin.

143

Painted wooden hinged altar (detail) from Ethiopia, around 1900. Museum für Völkerkunde, Dresden.

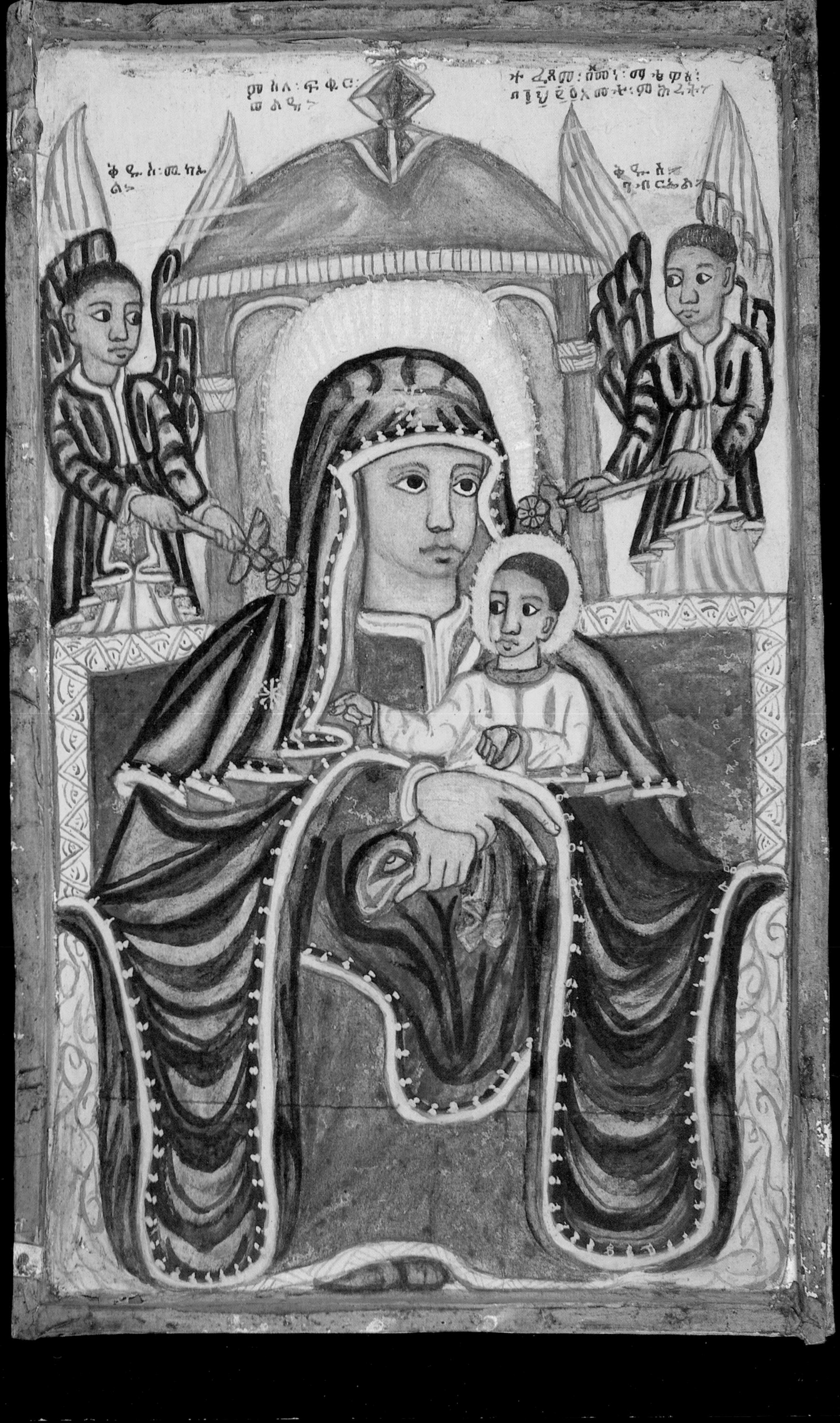
ምስለ፡ ፍቁር፡ ወልዳ
ቅዱስ፡ ሚካኤል
ቅዱስ፡ ገብርኤል

144

Figures of a moor and mooress as candleholders, so-called gueridons, ascribed to Balthasar Permoser. Lacquered wood, gilded silver, precious stones, mother-of-pearl. Early 18th century. Staatliche Kunstsammlungen Dresden.

145

Female mask. Rautenstrauch-Joest-Museum, Cologne.

146

Particularly colourful jewellery of a Masai woman.

servant next to *Bathsheba,* in his picture of that name dating from 1594. Peter Paul Rubens (1577–1640) put a dark-skinned female servant in the background of his *Toilette of Venus.* The motif of the female black servant reappears in Jean Auguste Dominique Ingres' (1780–1867) painting *The Odaliske,* and in the companion in Édouard Manet's (1832–1883) *Olympia.* Eugène Delacroix (1799–1863) painted *The Women of Algiers* in 1834, in which the pipe-smoking white women are being served by a negress.

Despite the discoveries made in the 15th and 16th centuries, right up to the 18th and 19th centuries little was known of Africa beyond the coastal areas. Portrayals of people were therefore largely products of the imagination of the artists. Giovanni Battista Tiepolo's (1696–1770) fresco *Africa,* on the ceiling of the Wurzburg Residence, a product of the late baroque and rococo period, depicts lively scenes. The pastel pictures of the Italian Rosalba Carriera (1675–1757) are especially worthy of mention. The artist received many commissions from Augustus the Strong, and in the Dresden collection there are 4 pastels representing allegories of the 4 continents known at the time: Europe, Asia, America and Africa. These allegories show the typical features of the various races—the African female is enveloped in mystery: "The dusky beauty is seductive; but dangers await whoever fails to resist the seduction and tries to penetrate the mysteries of the Dark Continent. The deadly vipers in the hands of the daughter of Africa serve as a warning"—thus the picture is described in a calendar. Clearly Rosalba Carriera's portrayal was also based on her imagination. The black beauty not only has her hands full of snakes, but also wears an unusual headwear, an elaborate turban decorated with the feathers of unknown birds, necklaces of enormous pearls, and a scorpion—admittedly as a decoration, but also as a further symbol of danger and mystery.

In 1800 the French artist Marie Guilhelmine Benoist (1768–1826) created her most famous picture *Portrait of a negress*—a work of enormous power.

147

Albrecht Dürer's drawing of *Katherina, aged 20 years* dates from 1521.

The thirsting after knowledge of the middle classes in the 18th and 19th centuries led to descriptions and portrayals of foreign lands and peoples in many books for children and young people. In his 12-volume womk *Picture Book for Children,* which appeared between 1790 and 1830, Friedrich Justin Bertuch devotes considerable space to Africa, with its "people and costumes". This children's encyclopedia from the era of Goethe aimed at disseminating humanistic descriptions and portrayals. And in the 19th century a number of moving humanistic portraits of African women were produced, like the painting *Negress with a Child in her Arms* by Eduard Hildebrandt (1818-1869). We see a woman who is carrying not only a child but also various tools and a basket, gazing proudly and confidently at us.

As colonialism spread and Africa was divided up among the European powers as a source of raw materials, the Africans now became of interest largely as workers. This shift of focus is reflected in the portrayals of Africans in caricatures—negroes with grotesque features, dusky women as objects for the lusts and desires of white men. This has, again, changed in the course of the 20th century, with its enormous social upheavals, and this trend is reflected in the trends of art the world over.

APPENDIX

Bibliography

List of the old travel reports and collections of travellers' reports by Arab, Italian, Portuguese, Danish, Dutch, French, English and American authors and the earlier literature on Africa, which is based on these reports (in chronological order)

1 IBN BATTUTA (Mohammed Ibn Abd Allah): *Travels in Asia and Africa, 1325 to 1354*. London, 1953.

2 AZURARA, G. E. DE (Zurara): *Chronica do descubrimento e conquista de Guiné, c. 1460*. Paris, 1841.

3 LEO AFRICANUS (Al-Hassan Ibn Muhammed al-Wassan): *Johann Leo's des Africaners Beschreibung von Africa*. Rome, 1526.

4 ALUARES, FRANCISCUS: *Franciscom Aluares Wahrhafftiger Bericht von den Landen / auch Geistlichem und Weltlichem Regiment / des Mechtigen Königs in Ethiopien / den wir Priester Johann nennen / wie solches durch die Kron Portugal mit besondern vleis erkundigt worden*. Eisleben, 1566.

5 FEYERABEND, SIEGMUND: *Wahrhafftige Beschreibung aller theil der Welt / darinn nicht allein etliche alte Landschaften / Königreich / Provintzen / Insuln / auch fürnehme Stedt und Märckte mit fleiß beschrieben werden / sondern auch sehr vil neuwe / so zu unsern zeiten / zu Wasser / durch vil sorgliche und vormals ungebrauchte Schiffarten / erfunden seyn*. Frankfurt, 1567.

6 LÓPEZ, ODOARDO: *Wahrhafftige und eigentliche Beschreibung des Königreiches Congo in Africa*. Part 1 to 5. (First published in Rome in 1591). Frankfurt/Main, 1597–1601.

7 MAREES, PIETER: *Beschryvinge ende Historische vershael van't Gant koninckrijk van Gunea anders de Goutcuste de Mina genaemt*. Amsterdam, 1602.

8 MEGISERIUS, HIERONYMUS: *Wahrhafftige / gründliche und ausführliche / so wol Historische alß Chorographische Beschreibung der überauss reichen / mechtigen und weitberühmten Insul Madagascar*. Altenburg, 1609.

9 ARNOLD, C.: *Von den Asiatischen, Africanischen und Americanischen Religionssachen*. Nuremberg, 1663.

10 DAPPER, OLFERT: *Beschreibung von Africa*. 2 vols. Amsterdam, 1670–71.

11 HIERONYMUS, P.: *P. Hieronymus, eines Jesuiten in Portugal, Neue Beschreibung und Bericht von der Beschaffenheit des Mohrenlandes, sonderlich des Abyssinischen Kaisertums*. 1st to 3rd part. Nuremberg, 1670.

12 MÜLLER, WILHELM JOHANN: *Die Africanische, auf der Guineischen Gold-Küste gelegene Landschaft Fetu*. Nuremberg, 1675.

13 CAVAZZI DA MONTECUCCOLO, G. A.: *Istorica descrittione d'etre Regnie Congo, Matambe e Angola*. Bologna, 1687.

14 BOSMAN, W.: *Nauwkeurige Beschreyoing van de Guinese Goud-Land an Sklave-Kust*. Utrecht, 1704.

15 ZUCCHELLI VON GRADISCA, P. ANTONIO: *Merckwürdige Missions- und Reisebeschreibung nach Congo in Ethiopien*. Frankfurt/Main, 1715.

16 *Allgemeine Historie der Reisen zu Wasser und zu Lande; oder Sammlung aller Reisebeschreibungen, welche bis itzo in verschiedenen Sprachen von allen Völkern herausgegeben werden*. 21 vols. Leipzig, 1741–1754.

17 *A new general collection of voyages and travels*. 7 vols. London, 1744–1747.

18 RÖMER, LUDEWIG FERDINAND: *Nachrichten von der Küste Guinea*. Copenhagen and Leipzig, 1769.

19 PROYART, LIÉVAIN BONAVENTURE: *Geschichte von Loango, Kakongo und anderen Königreichen in Afrika*. Leipzig, 1777.

20 DEMANET, ABBÉ: *Neue Geschichte des französischen Afrika*. 2 vols. Leipzig, 1778.

21 MATTHEW, JOHANN: *Reise nach Sierra Leone auf der westlichen Küste von Afrika. In Briefen, die der Verfasser während seines Aufenthaltes in diesem Lande, in den Jahren 1785, 1786 und 1787 an einen Freund in England schrieb*. Leipzig, 1789.

22 BRUCE, JOHN: *Travels between the years 1768 and 1773 into Abyssinia to discover the source of the Nile*. 5 vols. Edinburgh, 1790.

23 ISERT, PAUL HERMAN: *Reise nach Guinea und den Caribäischen Inseln in Kolumbien in Briefen an seine Freunde beschrieben.* Berlin/Leipzig, 1790.

24 CUHN, ERNST WILHELM: *Sammlung merkwürdiger Reisen in das Innere von Afrika.* Part 1 to 3. Leipzig, 1790–1791. Among others: *Reise nach dem Lande Bambouc mit genauen Nachrichten über die den Europäern noch unbekannten Goldbergwerke dieses Landes; Schreiben eines holländischen Offiziers aus dem Fort della Mina über die Sitten und Gebräuche der Einwohner dieser Küste, datiert 14. 6. 1787; Beschreibung von Nigritien. Aus dem Französischen des Herrn P, gewesenen Mitglieds des hohen Rats in Senegal und Kommandanten des Forts Saint Louis.*

25 *Neue Beiträge zur Kenntnis von Afrika. Unternehmungen der Gesellschaft zur Beförderung der Entdeckungen im Innern von Afrika und Robert Norries Reise in das Innere von Guinea.* Ed. by Johann Reinhold Forster. Berlin, 1791.

26 BRUNS, PAUL JACOB: *Versuch einer systematischen Erdbeschreibung der entferntesten Welttheile, Afrika, Asien, Amerika und Südindien.* Part 1 to 6. Frankfurt/Main and Nuremberg, 1791 to 1799.

27 EHRMANN, THEOPHIL FRIEDRICH: *Geschichte der merkwürdigsten Reisen, welche seit dem zwölften Jahrhundert zu Wasser und Lande unternommen worden sind.* 22 vols. Frankfurt, Main, 1791–1799.

28 LA SALLE, RITTER: *Reisen und Schicksale.* Leipzig, 1796.

29 WADSTRÖM, CARL BERNHARD: *Versuch über Kolonien vorzüglich in Rücksicht auf die westliche Küste von Afrika, nebst einer Beschreibung der bis jetzt dort errichteten Kolonien, besonders der neuen von Sierra Leone und Bulame.* 1st to 2nd part. Leipzig, 1796.

30 PARK, MUNGO: *Reisen im Innern von Afrika auf Veranstaltung der afrikanischen Gesellschaft in den Jahren 1795 bis 1797 unternommen.* Berlin, 1799.

31 JAILLES, DE LA: *Reise nach Senegal.* Hamburg/Mainz, 1802.

32 *Historische und philosophische Skizze der Entdeckungen und Niederlassungen der Europäer in Nord- und West-Afrika am Ende des 18. Jahrhunderts.* Ed. by Carl Steudel. Bremen, 1802.

33 DURAND, JEAN-BAPTIST-LÉONARD: *Nachrichten von den Senegal-Ländern.* Weimar, 1803.

34 *Neue Bibliothek der wichtigsten Reisebeschreibungen zur Erweiterung der Erd- und Völkerkunde.* Ed. by F. J. Bertuch. 41 vols. Weimar, 1815–1830.

35 RILEY, J.: *James Riley, Befehlshaber und Supercargo des Americanischen Kauffahrteischiffs Commerce. Schicksale und Reisen an der Westküste und im Innern von Africa in den Jahren 1815 und 1816, von ihm selbst beschrieben nebst Nachricht von Tombucto und der bisher unentdeckten großen Stadt Wassanah.* Jena, 1818.

36 MONRAD, H. C.: *Gemälde der Küste von Guinea und der Einwohner derselben, wie auch der Dänischen Kolonien auf dieser Küste; entworfen während meines Aufenthaltes in Afrika in den Jahren 1805 bis 1809.* Weimar, 1824.

37 DENHAM, DIXON, HUGH AND OUDNEY CLAPPERTON: *Beschreibung der Reise und Entdeckungen im nördlichen und mittleren Afrika in den Jahren 1822-1824.* Weimar, 1827.

38 *Taschenbibliothek der wichtigsten und interessantesten See- und Land-Reisen, von der Erfindung der Buchdruckerkunst bis auf unsere Zeiten.* Ed. by Joachim Heinrich Jäck. 27 vols. Nuremberg, 1827–1832.

39 LANDER, RICHARD AND JOHN: *Reise in Afrika zur Erforschung des Nigers bis zu seiner Mündung.* 1st to 3rd part. Leipzig, 1833.

40 HARRIS, WILLIAM CORNWALLIS: *Gesandtschaftsreise nach Schoa und Aufenthalt in Südabyssinien 1841-1843.* 1st to 3rd section. Stuttgart, Tübingen, 1845.

41 *Das Buch des Sudan oder Reisen des Scheich Zani el-Abidîn in Nigritien.* Ed. by Georg Rosen. Leipzig, 1847.

42 DUNCAN, JOHN: *Reisen in Westafrika von Wydah durch das Königreich Dahomey nach Adofudia im Innern.* 2 vols. Leipzig, 1848.

43 CRUICKSHANK, BRODIE: *Ein achtzehnjähriger Aufenthalt auf der Goldküste Afrika's.* Leipzig, 1855.

44 LENZ, OSKAR: *Skizzen aus Westafrika.* Berlin, 1877.

45 *Zur Geschichte Abessiniens im 17. Jahrhundert. Der Gesandtschaftsbericht des Hassan ben Ahmed El-Haimi.* Translated by F. E. Preiser. Berlin, 1898.

Further reading

46 ABEL, A.: *Les musulmans noirs du Maniema.* Brussels, 1960.

47 ABRAHAM, W. E.: *The mind of Africa.* London, 1962.

48 AKINJOGBIN, I. A.: *Dahomey and its neighbours (1708-1818).* London, 1967.

49 ANDERSSON, E.: *Messianic Popular Movements in the Lower Congo.* Uppsala, 1958.

50 ARNOLD, B.: "Frauendarstellungen in der 'Touristenkunst' Westafrikas", in: *Kleine Beiträge. Aus dem Staatlichen Museum für Völkerkunde Dresden.* Instalment 4. Dresden, 1981.

51 BAETA, C. G.: *Prophetism in Ghana.* London, 1962.

52 BALANDIER, G.: *Daily Life in the Kingdom of the Congo from the sixteenth to the eighteenth century.* London, 1968.

53 BAUMANN, H.: *Schöpfung und Urzeit im Mythos der afrikanischen Völker.* Berlin (West), 1964.

54 BECKMANN, J.: *Literatur der älteren Reisebeschreibungen.* 8 parts. Göttingen, 1807-1810.

55 BITTERLI, U.: *Die Entdeckung des schwarzen Afrikaners*. Zurich and Freiburg i. Br., 1970.

56 BITTERLI, U.: *Die "Wilden" und die "Zivilisierten". Grundzüge einer Geistes- und Kulturgeschichte der europäisch-überseeischen Begegnung*. Munich, 1976.

57 BLUME, M.-L.: *Medizin- und kunsthistorische Betrachtung der Geburtshilfe im Alten Ägypten und in Weiß- und Schwarzafrika*. Göttingen, 1968.

58 BLYDEN, E. W.: *Christianity, Islam and the Negro Race*. London, 1887.

59 BLYDEN, E. W.: *African Life and Customs*. London, 1908.

60 BLYDEN, E. W.: *The Negro in Ancient History*. Washington, 1969.

61 BRENTJES, B.: *Uraltes junges Afrika. 5000 Jahre afrikanischer Geschichte nach zeitgenössischen Quellen*. Berlin, no date.

62 BRENTJES, B.: *Fels- und Höhlenbilder Afrikas*. Leipzig, 1965.

63 BRINCKER, F.: *Wörterbuch des Otjiherero*. Leipzig, 1886.

64 BROCKELMANN, C.: *Geschichte der islamischen Völker und Staaten*. Munich, Berlin, 1939.

65 *Christianity in Tropical Africa*. Ed. by C. G. Baeta. New York, 1968.

66 DALZEL, A.: *Geschichte von Dahomey*. Leipzig, 1799.

67 DARK, P.: *Die Kunst von Benin*. Prague, 1960.

68 DAVIDSON, B.: *Alt-Afrika wiederentdeckt*. Berlin, 1962.

69 DEBRUNER, H.: "Ein Rousseau-Schüler in Afrika. Paul Herman Isert in Guinea 1783–1789," in: *Evangelisches Missions-Magazin*. Instalment 2. Basle, 1959.

70 DESCHAMPS, H.: *Les religions de l'Afrique Noire*. Paris, 1960.

71 DROST, D.: *Kunst aus Afrika. Museum für Völkerkunde zu Leipzig*. Leipzig, 1966.

72 DIETRICH, K.: *Byzantinische Quellen zur Länder- und Völkerkunde. 5. bis 15. Jahrhundert*. Leipzig, 1912.

73 ELIADE, M.: *Das Mysterium der Wiedergeburt. Initiationsriten, ihre kulturelle und religiöse Bedeutung*. Zurich and Stuttgart, 1961.

74 *Ethnographisches Mosaik. Museum für Völkerkunde Dresden*. Ed. by G. Guhr and P. Neumann. Berlin, 1982.

75 FAGG, W. P.: *Vergessene Negerkunst. Afro-portugiesisches Elfenbein*. Prague, 1959.

76 FORMAN, W., AND B. BRENTJES: *Afrikanische Plastik*. Leipzig, 1967.

77 FORMAN, W., B. FORMAN AND P. DARK: *Die Kunst von Benin*. Prague, 1966.

78 FROBENIUS, L.: *Die afrikanischen Felsbilder*. Graz, 1962.

79 FRÖHLICH, W.: *Das westafrikanische Elfenbeinhorn aus dem 16. Jahrhundert im Rautenstrauch-Joest-Museum*. Cologne, 1960.

80 FROELICH, J. S.: *Les musulmans d'Afrique Noir*. Paris, 1962.

81 GRIAULE, M.: *Masques Dogons*. Paris, 1938.

82 GRIAULE, M.: *Schwarze Genesis. Ein afrikanischer Schöpfungsbericht*. Freiburg, Basle, Vienna, 1970.

83 GRUBE, A. W.: *Bilder aus Afrika. Nach vorzüglichen Reisebeschreibungen*. Stuttgart, 1925.

84 HARLEY, G. W.: *Native African Medicine*. London, 1970.

85 HASELBERGER, H.: *Bautraditionen der westafrikanischen Negerkulturen*. Vienna, 1964.

86 HEINE, I.: *Die Stellung der Frauen in der Wirtschaft Westafrikas*. Münster, 1973.

87 HIMMELHEBER, H.: *Negerkunst und Negerkünstler*. Brunswick, 1960.

88 HIMMELHEBER, U.: *Schwarze Schwester. Von Mensch zu Mensch in Afrika*. Bremen, 1957.

89 HIRSCHBERG, W.: *Völkerkunde Afrikas*. Mannheim, 1964.

90 HIRSCHBERG, W.: *Die Kulturen Afrikas*. Frankfurt/Main, 1974.

91 HOWE, R. W.: *Black Africa. Africa South of Sahara from Prehistory to Independence*. New York, 1966.

92 IHLE, A.: *Das alte Königreich Kongo*. Leipzig, 1929.

93 JAHN, J.-H.: *Wir nannten sie Wilde. Aus alten und neuen Reisebeschreibungen*. Munich, 1964.

94 JAHN, J.-H.: *Geschichte der neoafrikanischen Literatur. Eine Einführung*. Düsseldorf, Cologne, 1966.

95 JUNGWIRTH, W.: *Benin in den Jahren 1485–1700. Ein Kultur- und Geschichtsbild*. Vienna, 1968.

96 KI-ZERBO, J.: *Die Geschichte Schwarz-Afrikas*. Wuppertal, 1979.

97 KOHL, K. H.: *Entzauberter Blick. Das Bild vom Guten Wilden und die Erfahrung der Zivilisation*. Berlin, 1981.

98 KOHL-LARSEN, L. AND M.: *Die Bilderstrasse Ostafrikas. Felsbilder in Tanganyika*. Eisenach, Kassel, 1958.

99 KOSSODO, B. L.: *Die Frau in Afrika. Zwischen Tradition und Befreiung*. Munich, 1979.

100 LEBLANC, M.: *Personalité de la femme Katangaise*. Brussels, Paris, 1960.

101 LEE, S.: *Travels of Ibn Battuta*. London, 1829.

102 LEISKANDL, H.: *Edle Wilde, Heiden und Barbaren. Fremdheit als Bewertungskriterium zwischen Kulturen.* Vienna, 1966.

103 LEITH-ROSS, S.: *African Women.* London, 1939.

104 LHOTE, H.: *Die Felsbilder der Sahara.* Würzburg, 1958.

105 LITTMANN, E.: *The Legend of the Queen of Sheba in the Tradition of Axum.* Leiden, 1904.

106 LOMMEL, A.: *Masken, Gesichter der Menschheit.* Zurich, 1970.

107 MAHMUD, SAYYID FAYYAZ: *Geschichte des Islam.* Munich, 1964.

108 MARIE-ANDRÉ DU SACRÉ CŒUR: *La femme noire en Afrique Occidentale.* Paris, 1939.

109 MBITI, J. S.: *Afrikanische Religion und Weltanschauung.* Berlin (West), 1974.

110 MEINHOF, C.: *Die Dichtung der Afrikaner.* Berlin, 1911.

111 MIRIMANOV, B.: *Kunst der Urgesellschaft und traditionelle Kunst Afrikas und Ozeaniens.* Dresden/Moscow, 1973.

112 MITCHEL, R. C., AND H. W. TURNER: *A comprehensive bibliography of modern African religious movements.* Evanton, 1966.

113 MUTHESIUS, A.: *Die Afrikanerin.* Düsseldorf, 1959.

114 *Mythen der Völker.* 3 vols. Ed. by P. Grimal. Frankfurt/Main, Hamburg, 1967.

115 MZIK, H. V.: *Die Reise des Arabers Ibn Battuta nach Indien und China.* Hamburg, 1911.

116 NIANE, D. T.: *Soundjata. Ein Mandingo-Epos.* Leipzig, 1975.

117 PARRINDER, E. G.: *African Traditional Religion.* London, 1954.

118 PARRINDER, E. G.: *Religion in Africa.* New York, 1969.

119 PAULITSCHKE, P.: *Die geographische Erforschung des afrikanischen Kontinents von den ältesten Zeiten bis auf unsere Tage.* Vienna, 1880.

120 PAULITSCHKE, P.: *Die Afrika-Literatur von 1500 bis 1750.* Vienna, 1882.

121 PLOSS, H.: *Das Weib in der Natur- und Völkerkunde.* 2 vols. Leipzig, 1887.

122 PRIETZE, R.: *Haussa-Sprichwörter und Haussa-Lieder.* Kirchhain, 1904.

123 RACHEWITZ, B. DE: *Afrikanische Kunst.* Zurich, 1960.

124 RATTRAY, P.: *Ashanti Law and Condition.* London, 1958.

125 REHWALDT, H.: *Geheimbünde in Afrika.* Munich, 1941.

126 REITZENSTEIN, F.: *Das Weib bei den Naturvölkern.* Berlin, 1923.

127 SCOBIE, A.: *Women of Africa.* London, 1960.

128 SMIRNOVA, R. M.: *Polozheniye zhenshchin v stranakh Afriki.* Moscow, 1967.

129 SOW, A. I.: *La femme, la vache, la Foi.* Paris, 1966.

130 SUCKOW, C.: *Die Bantu- und Khoisanbevölkerung Südafrikas im Spiegel der Berichte deutscher Reisender.* Berlin, 1973.

131 SULZMANN, E.: "Die Bewegung der Antonier im alten Reich Kongo", in: *Mühlmann, W. E., Chiliasmus und Nativismus.* Berlin (West), 1961.

132 THURNWALD, H.: *Die schwarze Frau im Wandel Afrikas.* Stuttgart, 1935.

133 TRIMINGHAM, J. S.: *Islam in West Africa.* Oxford, 1959.

134 TSHEBOKSAROV, N. N., AND I. A. TSHEBOKSAROVA: *Völker, Rassen, Kulturen.* Leipzig, Jena, Berlin, 1979.

135 TURNER, H. W.: *History of an African independent Church.* Part 1 and 2. Oxford, 1967.

136 VERMOT-MANGOLD, R.: *Die Rolle der Frau bei den Kabre in Nord-Togo.* Basle, 1977.

137 WESTERMANN; D.: *Geschichte Afrikas.* Cologne, 1952.

138 *Wie sie sich sahen. Das Menschenbild in der Kunst ferner Völker.* Ed. by Staatliches Museum für Völkerkunde Dresden. Dresden, 1976.

139 WOLF, S.: *Afrikanische Elfenbeinlöffel des 16. Jahrhunderts im Museum für Völkerkunde Dresden.* Cologne, 1960.

140 *Women in Tropical Africa.* Ed. by D. Paulme. London, 1963.

141 ZWERNEMANN, J.: *Die Bedeutung von Himmels- und Erdgott in westafrikanischen Religionen.* Mainz, 1954.

Index

Sources of illustrations

Deutsche Fotothek, Dresden 40,
41, 42, 43, 52, 57, 63, 64, 65,
71, 87, 94, 95, 96, 99, 100,
105, 147
F. A. Brockhaus Verlag, Leipzig
31, 66, 90, 93, 98, 124, 138
Forschungsbibliothek Gotha 17,
18, 47, 48, 49, 50, 51, 53, 54,
55, 70, 72, 73, 74, 76, 77, 89,
103, 106
Harald Lange, Leipzig 146
Historisches Museum Bern 10,
121, 132, 139

Institut für Denkmalpflege,
Berlin 11, 12, 13, 14, 142
Musée national, Paris 4
Museum für Völkerkunde,
Dresden 23, 27, 33, 34, 58,
83, 102, 119, 143
Museum für Völkerkunde,
Frankfurt/Main 15, 20, 22,
78, 117, 118
Museum für Völkerkunde,
Hamburg 56, 61, 62, 82, 88,
104, 115, 126, 130, 131,
140
Museum für Völkerkunde, Staat-
liche Museen Preussischer
Kulturbesitz, Berlin (West)
25, 26, 29, 67, 97

Museum für Völkerkunde,
Vienna 5, 122, 125
National Museum of Denmark,
Copenhagen 3
Publisher's archives 9, 16, 19,
28, 35, 39, 44, 79, 81, 85, 86,
101, 120, 127, 135, 141, 144
Rautenstrauch-Joest-Museum,
Cologne 36, 60, 84, 92, 109,
112, 113, 114, 133, 136, 137,
145
Rietbergmuseum, Zurich 1, 2,
21, 24, 30, 68
Staatliches Museum für Völker-
kunde, Linden-Museum,
Stuttgart 6, 8, 32, 37, 38, 59,
69, 80, 108, 110, 116, 123

Tropical Museum, Amsterdam
7, 91, 129
Völkerkundemuseum of the
University of Zurich 107,
111, 128, 134

The following illustrations were
drawn from motifs in books:
Ill. 45 *Meyers Lexikon*. Vol. 3,
p. 261. Leipzig, 1972.
Ill. 46 *Meyers Lexikon*. Vol. 1,
p. 326. Leipzig, 1972.
Ill. 75 *Meyers Lexikon*. Vol. 5,
p. 184. Leipzig, 1973.
Map p. 6 *Atlas zur Geschichte*.
Vol. 1, p. 55 II. Gotha/Leipzig,
1973.